PRAISE

Mark D... ... ... of the great teachers!
REV. MARY OMWAKE, LEADERSHIP COUNCIL,
ASSOCIATION FOR GLOBAL NEW THOUGHT

Without Mark David's inspiration, example and encouragement, I might never have had the courage to publish my book.
NANCY POGUE LATURNER, AUTHOR OF "VOLUNTARY NOMADS"

The Q'ntana Trilogy Books
The MoonQuest, The StarQuest, The SunQuest

Leaves you turning every single page, hungry for more!
DAVID MICHAEL, AUTHOR OF "THE UNITED SERIES"

An enjoyable journey into a wondrous world that will leave you yearning to return again and again.
JUDY SMITH ADAMS, SPRINGFIELD, MISSOURI

An intriguing and exhilarating magical tale.
DAN STONE, AUTHOR OF "THE REST OF OUR LIVES"

Also by Mark David Gerson
Acts of Surrender: A Writer's Memoir
Dialogues with the Divine: Encounters with My Wisest Self
The Book of Messages: Writings Inspired by Melchizedek

A dynamic read for the creative spirit within each of us. Positive inspiration at its best.
HANK BRUCE, AUTHOR OF "PEACE BEYOND ALL FEAR: A TRIBUTE TO JOHN DENVER'S VISION"

A book that has the power to awaken, empower and inspire anyone who reads it.
MELISSA SHAWN, AUSTIN, TEXAS

A masterful work from one of today's masters.
JOAN CERIO, AUTHOR OF "HARDWIRED TO HEAVEN"

Mark David Gerson's Resources for Writers

The Voice of the Muse: Answering the Call to Write
From Memory to Memoir: Writing the Stories of Your Life
Organic Screenwriting: Writing for Film, Naturally
Writer's Block Unblocked:
Seven Surefire Ways to Free Up Your Writing and Creative Flow
The Voice of the Muse Companion: Guided Meditations for Writers (recording)

*Whenever I feel blocked, I open this book,
read a couple of pages and feel inspired again.*
ANNA BLAGOSLAVOVA, MOSCOW, RUSSIA

Makes writer's block obsolete!
DR. BRENT POTTER, AUTHOR OF "BORDERLINE PERSONALITY DISORDER"

Every writer can gain a solid dose of insight and inspiration from this book.
W. TERRY WHALIN, AUTHOR OF "JUMPSTART YOUR PUBLISHING DREAMS"

No matter where you are on your creative journey or what writing demons you may be wrestling with, you'll be so glad you read this book.
JULIE ISAAC, AUTHOR OF "THE TOP TEN TIPS
TO UNLEASH YOUR BOOK WRITING GENIUS"

A skilled magician, Mark David Gerson is able to draw reluctant words out of even the most blocked writer.
CHRISTOPHER KEMP, CHATHAM, NEW JERSEY

With this book Mark David Gerson goes even further to secure his position in the literary world as the best friend a writer ever had.
LUKE YANKEE, AUTHOR OF "JUST OUTSIDE THE SPOTLIGHT"

An engaging, almost meditative journey filled with valuable lessons for all writers, not just those working on movies.
CASEY RYAN, HOST OF "THE CUTTING ROOM FLOOR"

A seminal work that should be read carefully by any and all aspiring writers for film and television ... an enduringly useful reference work.
"THE MIDWEST BOOK REVIEW"

Birthing Your Book

even if you don't know what it's about!

Mark David Gerson

BIRTHING YOUR BOOK
EVEN IF YOU DON'T KNOW WHAT IT'S ABOUT!

Copyright © 2015 Mark David Gerson
All rights reserved
No part of this book may be reproduced, stored in a retrieval system or transmitted by any means, electronic, mechanical, photocopying, recording or otherwise, without written permission from the publisher, except for the inclusion of brief quotations in critical reviews and certain other noncommercial uses permitted by copyright law.

Published in association with MDG Media International
www.mdgmediainternational.com

ISBN-13: 978-1502368119
ISBN-10: 1502368110

Cover Photograph: Kathleen Messmer *www.kathleenmessmer.com*

Coming Soon:
An Epic Motion Picture Trilogy
from Mark David Gerson's Books!

The MoonQuest Movie: The Q'ntana Trilogy, Part I
The StarQuest Movie: The Q'ntana Trilogy, Part II
The SunQuest Movie: The Q'ntana Trilogy, Part III

More information at www.markdavidgerson.com

Find your passion and embrace it. Passionately.
Mark David Gerson

To the books I have birthed
and to those I have yet to conceive.
And to my daughter:
the best, brightest
and most beautiful birth ever.

Contents

Gratitude		11
Opening Words		13
1. Getting Started		15
You Have a Book in You	17	
How to Use Birthing Your Book	19	
First Steps	21	
2. Meet Your Muse		23
The Truth About Your Muse	25	
Write with Ease on the Muse Stream	27	
"Help! I'm Stuck!"	29	
Write with Ease on the Muse Stream: A Meditative Experience	33	
Meet Your Muse: A Guided Meditation	35	
3. Conception		39
Pre-Conception	41	
Revelations	43	
The Soul of Your Book	45	
Your Ocean of Stories	47	
Your Ocean of Stories: A Guided Meditation	49	
In the Beginning Was the Word	51	
Keys to Your Kingdom of Creation	53	
Fifty Keys to Your Book's Conception and Creation		
Birth of a Book	57	
Birthing Your Book: A Meditative Journey	59	
4. Mark David's "Rules" for Birthing Your Book		63
Twenty Rules for Birthing Your Book	65	
Rule #1: There Are No Rules	67	
The Power of Now	69	
Do You Know What Your Book Is About?	71	
"I Don't Know How to Start (or Finish) My Book"	73	
Forget Everything You Think You Know About Writing	75	

Go Boldly	*77*
The Naked Truth	*79*
Your Book Is Smarter Than You Are	*81*
Tales of the Unexpected	*83*
Relax: It's Only Your First (or Second or Third) Draft	*85*
Your Book is Out of Order	*87*
Kicking the Perfectionism Habit	*89*
The Voice of Discernment	*91*
Is Your Write Book the Right Book?	*93*
It's Not Always Time to Write	*95*
What Do Publishers Want?	*97*
Write. Right?	*99*
Are Your Goals Working for You?	*101*
Acts of Commitment	*103*
Rules? What Rules?	*105*

5. Creation   107

Genesis	*109*
Your Book Chose You	*111*
Writing Through the Fog	*113*
Write What You Know?	*115*
Trust Your Book	*117*
Talk to Your Book: A Meditative Journey	*119*
Inside Your Book: A Guided Meditation	*121*
The Coppola Method	*125*
First Drafts	*127*
Let Judgment Go: A Guided Meditation	*129*

6. Craft   133

Take Your Time	*135*
Into the Heart of Discipline	*137*
Whose Book Are You Writing?	*139*
To Outline or Not to Outline?	*141*
The Word Tree	*143*
Word Pictures	*145*
Know Your World	*147*
Populating the Worlds of Your Book	*151*
Painting the Worlds of Your Book	*153*
Driven to Distraction?	*157*
Read to Write, Read to Live	*161*

7. Vision — 163

What's Your Vision for Your Book? — 165
  My Vision Statement for The Voice of the Muse
  My Vision Statement for Acts of Surrender
  My Vision Statement for the Q'ntana Screenplays and Stage Musicals
Vision Quest: A Guided Meditation — 167

8. Revision — 171

Reclaiming the "Vision" in Revision — 173
Entering into the Spirit of Revision — 175
Mark David's Rules for Revision — 179
Trust Your Vision, Trust Your Book — 185

9. Going Public — 187

Remember Your Vision Statement? — 189
Author Support — 191
Reaching Out for Feedback — 195
  The Seven Be's of Empowered Feedback
  The Seven Be's of Compassionate Feedback
Rising Above Rejection — 199
Rejected? You're Not the Only One! — 201

10. Living Your Book — 203

The Story Knows Best — 205
Mark David's Rules for Living a Creative Life — 207
Trust. Let Go. Leap. — 211

11. Parting Words — 213

It's Time to Live the Dream — 215
You Are a Writer: A Guided Meditation — 217
Your Book, Your Journey — 219
Endings and Beginnings — 221

More from Mark David Gerson — 222

The MoonQuest: The Q'ntana Trilogy, Book I — 222
Acts of Surrender: A Writer's Memoir — 223

Gratitude

My first *Birthing Your Book* acknowledgment goes to a creation of my unconscious mind, a dream character named Beth. Without Beth's forceful urging, I could not now be writing these words, words that result from some twenty years of teaching.

Beth turned up early one morning more than two decades ago, a few days after Carole H. Leckner, my then-mentor, invited me to teach a section of the writing course she had created. This was Carole's third invitation; I had turned down the first two.

In the dream, Beth is seriously injured when her jeep strikes a land mine. Later in her hospital room, her husband begs her not to teach. "It's too dangerous," he argues.

"I must," Beth counters.

When I woke up from the dream, I knew that I, too, had no choice but to teach.

Thus, my second expression of gratitude goes to Carole. Teaching her University of Toronto writing course led to workshops of my own, workshops that birthed books I didn't know I had in me, including those I knew nothing about as I began to write them. All those experiences contributed to this book.

To the participants of those many classes, seminars and workshops over the years, thank you. I have learned at least as much from you as I have endeavored to teach. As well, your enthusiastic response to my offerings continues to spur me on — in my writing as well as in my teaching.

Every writer needs a personal cheerleading squad, especially on those days when self-esteem is in shreds and feelings of futility are rampant. Among my most steadfast cheerleaders are Adam Bereki, Joan Cerio, Sander Dov Freedman, Kathleen Messmer and Karen Weaver. A special shoutout goes to Luann Wolfe, without whose encouragement this book would not likely exist.

Thank you, too, to my many online friends and followers for reminding that I am part of a community of writers and readers and for also reminding me of the motivational power of my words.

I write these acknowledgments, as I have written so much of this book and my others, surrounded by the caffeinated buzz of a Starbucks. To the baristas of this and so many other cafes in various parts of the U.S., thank you for the welcome fuel and the creativity-enhancing ambience, as well as for your patience with the demands of this sometimes eccentric author.

If most of this book was birthed in the shadow of Albuquerque's majestic Sandia Mountains, bits and pieces of it had their origins in settings as disparate as Sedona, Santa Fe, Toronto, Hawaii, and the empty stretch of US-93 between Kingman, Arizona and Las Vegas. To all those places, and others too numerous to mention, thank you for continuing to inspire me, not only in my writing but in my life.

Finally, to my Muse: Thank you for your forbearance as I grow, not always gracefully, into deeper surrender to you and to the infinite well of stories that resides within me.

Opening Words

- *I know I have a book in me; I just don't know what it's about.*
- *I have a great idea for a book, but I don't know how to start.*
- *I started this book, but now I'm stuck.*
- *I've been told I should write a book, but I don't know what to write.*
- *I've been told I need to write a book, but I don't know how to write it.*
- *I have all these stories in me. How do I turn them into a book?*
- *I really want to write a book, but I have no ideas.*
- *I have too many ideas. How do I pick one to write about?*
- *How can I write a book? I'm not a writer.*

If any of these sound familiar, you're in the right place. You can now stop worrying about whether you can write a book…or even write. You can stop wondering what to write or how to write it. You can stop worrying about how to begin. You can stop wondering whether you can keep your momentum going until the end. You can stop worrying. Period.

It doesn't matter whether you're a seasoned writer or just starting out. It doesn't matter whether you're writing in a familiar genre or whether you're feeling called to something new. It doesn't even matter whether you know what your book is about.

In the chapters ahead, I will offer you dynamic tools to get you started and keep you writing. I will serve up compelling inspiration to help you stay motivated, committed and impassioned. And I will guide you through exercises and experiences guaranteed to spark new ideas or expand on existing ones or, where relevant, unveil for you your book's thrust and content.

Through it all I will show you how easy it can be to birth your book, even if you don't know what it's about.

What if it's not a book you feel called to write? What if it's a screenplay or stage play, an essay or blog post, a short story or poem? What if it's something more technical, like a research paper or dissertation? Although I focus mostly on book-writing here, nearly everything you will read in *Birthing Your Book* applies equally to any of those other forms. And although I use the word "story" to describe your content, my definition of story is broad enough to include anything and everything you might write, regardless of its medium, form or genre.

One thing *Birthing Your Book* is not is a step-by-step how-to. When it comes to creativity, I don't believe in step-by-step how-to's or, as you will soon discover, in rules. Rather, it's a guided journey that will reawaken you to the creative vision, intuitive wisdom and expressive power you already possess — qualities that are as natural to you as is your DNA.

It's that vision that will reveal your book to you, if you let it. It's that wisdom that will write your book for you, if you let it. It's that expressive power that, if you surrender to it, will translate the stories of your heart into stories for every heart…that will birth your book onto the page for all to experience.

So turn the page, and let the birthing begin!

Mark David Gerson
October 2014

1. Getting Started

Respond to every call that excites your spirit.
RUMI, POET/MYSTIC

The scariest moment is always just before you start.
STEPHEN KING, NOVELIST

You Have a Book in You

You have a book in you. Perhaps you have sensed this book for forever. Perhaps it has only recently made itself known to you. Perhaps your sole awareness of it comes from others who insist that it's there. Or perhaps this book still lurks in the shadowy recesses of your unconscious mind, not yet ready to let itself be glimpsed.

Maybe you already suspect what this book might be about. Or maybe your opening page is not only empty of words but empty of ideas.

Regardless, you do have a book in you. You have a book in you not because you are unusual (though your stories may be), but because we are all storytellers. We each carry an infinite potential for self-expression-through-story that, if we open to it, can reshape our lives and the lives of others in ways we cannot begin to imagine.

It's true for you. It's true for me. It's true for everyone.

It's true, too, for the eighty-two percent of Americans who say they plan to write a book someday. Will you be one of the majority for whom that "someday" never comes? Or are you one of the few ready to launch the journey of a lifetime: the journey into an experience of your storyteller self? Into an experience of your own creativity?

The good news is that the birth of your book need be neither painful nor laborious.

Here's more good news: Whether you are conscious of it or not, you already know what your book is about, how to start it, how to finish it and how to fill in all the middle stuff.

Here's even more good news: Your book already exists. It resides, full and complete, in that same realm in which your dreams reside...in that dimension somewhere beyond the three we know, beyond the fourth of time as well. It exists in that miracle-filled kingdom where everything is possible. It exists in your heart.

My job is to guide you to all those places within you where your book waits for you to acknowledge it, access it and make it manifest...where it has waited since the beginning of time to find its expression on the page through you.

Your job is to listen, trust and surrender — not to me, but to the voice of your book, the voice of your Muse, the voice of your inner vision, the voice of your heart.

They speak to you now. Are you ready to hear and heed what they have to say? Of course you are. That's why you are here. That's why I am here. And that's why this book I knew little about, other than its title, birthed itself through me for you.

How to Use *Birthing Your Book*

There are no rules for birthing your book as I will remind you frequently in these pages. There is no right way and no wrong way. There is only the way that works for you, today.

Given that, why would I insist that you read *Birthing Your Book* straight through to the end, the way you read most other writing books? After all, I didn't write it that way. Rather, as I do with all my books for writers, I encourage you to use this book however it calls you to. If you choose not to follow the progression I have laid out for you, then flip to any page at random and trust that it will present the inspirational nugget or exercise perfectly suited to your book-birthing needs of the moment.

All I suggest is that early in your explorations you visit "Write with Ease on the Muse Stream" in Section 2, as it presents the philosophies that underlie not only this book but all my work.

Consider, too, keeping a *Birthing Your Book* journal. Use it, of course, for the exercises and explorations scattered throughout the book; it may prove helpful to have all those writings recorded in a single place. Use it as well for notes about your book-in-progress, to record your impressions and experiences of our journey together, and to release whatever anxieties and frustrations show up along the way.

Birthing Your Book also includes a series of guided meditations and meditative journeys to help you discover the theme and thrust of your book, express your vision for it more eloquently and make your book-writing experience more natural, free-flowing and spontaneous.

There are several ways you can use them:
- Record them yourself for playback.
- Have a friend or writing partner read them to you, then return the favor.
- Get yourself into a quiet space and place, program your music player for five to forty-five minutes of contemplative music (depending on the length of the exercise) and read the meditation slowly and receptively, following its directions and suggestions.

If you prefer a more professionally guided approach, I have recorded five of this book's meditations:
- Meet Your Muse (Section 2)

- Your Ocean of Stories (Section 3)
- Let Judgment Go (Section 5)
- Vision Quest (Section 7)
- You Are a Writer (Section 11)

You'll find all five (along with an additional five not in *Birthing Your Book*) on *The Voice of the Muse Companion: Guided Meditations for Writers*, available on CD or as an MP3 download from Amazon, iTunes, Google Play and other online music sellers.

It's time now to move forward with birthing *your* book. Are you ready? Of course you are! Before we start, thought, I'd like you to get a pen, an envelope and a couple of index cards or pieces of paper. You've got them? Great! Let's take our first steps.

First Steps

- *What do you know right now about the book you feel called to write?*
- *Where are you now with that book, with your writing?*
- *How do you see yourself today, as the writer and author you are?*

Don't answer with your conscious mind. Instead, close your eyes and let a single word or phrase emerge that describes where you feel yourself to be in this moment…where your book is…where you both are, together.

Don't censor or second-guess what bubbles up into your awareness. Let it be whatever it is, however little conventional sense it seems to make in this moment

Whatever it is, note it on your piece of paper or index card next to the question, "Where am I now with my book?" or, if you have a working title, "Where am I now with [Title of book]?"

Don't question what comes up. Don't dismiss it. Just record it, without judgment.

Now, consider these additional questions from that same place of openness and non-judgment:

- What do I want from *Birthing Your Book*? What are my hopes? My desires? My expectations?
- Where would I like to be on the last page of *Birthing Your Book* that I am not in this moment?

Take a few minutes to jot down some notes on your piece of paper or index card. Record those hopes, those desires, those expectations. Let it be a few words, a few sentences or a few pages. Let it be whatever you need it to be. Let it express whatever you opened this book seeking.

When you're finished, sign it, date it and place it in your envelope. Seal the envelope and secure it to the inside back cover of this book or your *Birthing Your Book* journal, or secrete it somewhere else that is safe and out of sight, and forget about it.

You have taken your first steps. Now it's time to leap forward on your book-birthing journey.

2. Meet Your Muse

*I never exactly made a book.
It's rather like taking dictation.
I was given things to say.*
C.S. LEWIS, NOVELIST

Inspiration is just another word for heart.
CARSON MORTON, NOVELIST

The Truth About Your Muse

In Greek mythology, the nine Muses were the daughters of gods Zeus and Mnemosyne. Goddesses in their own right, each Muse presided over an aspect of the arts and sciences — from history to hymns, comedy to poetry and astronomy to tragedy.

Today, whether or not personified by a woman, the Muse has come to symbolize creative inspiration for all artists. Or, as I put it in the "Meet Your Muse" meditation later in this section, your Muse is "the being that…embodies your purest creative source, that font of creative energy, inspiration and revelation that we all have within us."

Many writers view their Muse as a capricious adversary that makes itself available somewhat reluctantly and only when conditions are perfect. "My muse has deserted me," writers complain. Or, "My Muse refuses to cooperate." Or, "My Muse is shy."

Those writers have it all wrong. Muses are never shy. It's writers who are deaf or, rather, choose not to listen. Muses are never uncooperative. It's writers who refuse to cooperate. Muses never desert, hold back or resist. Writers desert, hold back and resist all the time.

In those moments when you believe your Muse is not working with you, ask yourself these questions:

- Where am I, in truth, unwilling to work with my Muse?
- What is it about my book that I am unwilling to hear?
- What am I refusing to write?
- What am I reluctant to face within myself that is holding me back from writing my book?
- Which belief or way of life is my Muse challenging?
- How is my resistance to change and inner growth holding me back from moving forward with my book?
- Where am I not surrendering unconditionally to my Muse and to the book it is calling on me to write?
- Where else in my life or my creativity do I have resistance?

Try This

Open your journal and explore those questions as honestly as you dare, using the Muse Stream techniques described in the next chapter if you feel any resistance to accessing and expressing the truths of your heart. As you move forward with your book from the answers, you will never encounter a shy, uncooperative Muse again.

Write with Ease on the Muse Stream

Now we know what a Muse is. But what's a Muse Stream? Well, if you're familiar with terms like "free writing," "automatic writing," "stream of consciousness writing" or "morning pages," you already have a sense of what the Muse Stream is about: a wholesale, uncensored, right-brain outpouring onto the page. While those other techniques are used primarily as personal-growth exercises or to prime your creative pump, the Muse Stream is more than that. It's a practical tool that can get your book started and finished — from first to final draft.

In short, the Muse Stream is the free-flowing river of creative output that we all aspire to in our writing. It's the place where our books reside. It's the place where writer's block not only does not exist but cannot exist. It's the place where doubt and uncertainty cannot survive. When we allow ourselves to write from there, it's the place where the words tumble unhindered onto the page as swiftly as the waters of a stream down their channel.

The good news is that, contrary to conventional belief (and, perhaps, to your experience) that free-flow is available to you in every moment on any book project, even if you start out knowing little or nothing about it.

Not surprisingly, the key to that unstoppable flow is to write without stopping. Without stopping and without thinking.

Too often, we overthink as we write. We think and we worry. We think about where the next word is going to come from. We worry whether we're writing the "right" word. We think about spelling, punctuation and grammar. We worry about form and structure. We worry about what our book is about. We wonder how it will be received. We think about paragraph breaks, chapter breaks, coffee breaks.

Let's return for a moment to our swiftly moving stream. The water rushes from source to outlet in a frothy whoosh of easy flow, nothing impeding its forward progress. Now, drop a couple of boulders in its path and watch them hinder that flow. Drop a few more, and you no longer have any flow at all.

Each of your thoughts while you write can be one of those boulders. The more worry or anxiety linked to that thought, the bigger the boulder…and the more daunting the potential barrier.

Here's what's going on: For the most part, we think with the logical, controlling, analytical, critical side of our brain and write with the creative, imaginative, free-flowing side of our brain. And for the most part, when we do the former, we stunt the latter. When we stop to edit or plan or research or engage our "thinking" mind in any way, we also give voice to our inner critic, that nattering monkey mind determined to control a creative process that by its nature is inherently uncontrollable.

Why am I telling you all this? Because I am encouraging you to write your book on the Muse Stream. I am inviting you to dive into the Muse Stream and surrender to its flow.

Surrendering to the Muse Stream is about knowing that your book already exists whole and complete in some other realm. It's about trusting enough to let your fingers dance across the keyboard (or waltz across the page with your pen) as they release onto the blank sheet the words, sentences, paragraphs and pages that will reveal your book's already existent form.

How? It's simpler than you think. As you write…

- Don't stop to correct spelling punctuation or grammar. There is a time for editing, revising and correcting. That time is *not* in the midst of your creative flow.
- Don't stop to grope for the word that's on the tip of your tongue or to search for synonyms. Leave a blank space or type *xxxx* and keep writing.
- Don't stop to research perceived holes in your narrative. Insert a brief note about what's missing, set aside separate time for research and write on.
- Don't stop to structure your book, to figure out its theme or to plan, plot or organize its contents. Keep your pen or fingers moving and trust that the innate wisdom of your book will make itself known to you as you write.
- Don't stop for any of life's distractions. Keep your writing space and time as distraction-free as you can. (Need help with this? See "Driven to Distraction?" in Section 6.)
- Don't stop to think, worry or stress.
- Don't stop — for anything.

Write without stopping and no boulder will ever be able to divert your Muse Stream.

How do you start if you don't know what your book is about? That's a great question, one I will be answering it in the next sections.

What if you are able to get started but then find yourself stuck? Another great question. I'll answer that one right now.

"Help! I'm Stuck!"

There are many reasons why you might find yourself stranded on a shoal in the midst of your book's Muse Stream flow.
- Are you feeling overwhelmed by how little you know about the book you feel called to write?
- Are you trying to plan, plot or outline your book, rather than listening for its wisdom on the Muse Stream?
- Are you listening to your inner critic, your frightened inner child or the echoes of those who have judged or criticized you, rather than to the voice of your Muse and the voice of your book?
- Are you avoiding an emotionally or technically challenging chapter, section or book?
- Are you finding it difficult to continue without additional research?
- Are you afraid of hurting or offending someone with what you feel called to write?
- Are you overthinking this part of your book?
- Are you second-guessing yourself? Judging or censoring yourself?

Whichever it is, don't stop writing. Keep your pen moving or your fingers typing. It doesn't matter what you write, even if it's gibberish or something unrelated to the book at hand. It may feel foolish in the moment, but it's guaranteed to carry you through and past most fear and all hesitation. Write — anything — and before you know it, you will be back in a free and easy flow.

If you get stuck — we all do — here are ten ways to reignite your creative fire, free up your Muse Stream and keep the words of your book flowing easily onto the page.

1. Repeat

Repeat *anything* to keep your pen or keyboard in motion. Repeat the last word or sentence your wrote. Repeat the first sentence of the previous paragraph. Repeat the first sentence of your day's writing. Write/repeat anything, even if it's "I don't know what to write" or "This feels dumb" or "Repetition is silly" or "Why do I have to write this book?"

Keep repeating whatever you're repeating until the flow starts up again, and it will. Later, you can discard the words, phrases and sentences that have no place in your manuscript. Some, you might be surprised to discover, will remain.

2. Free-Associate

Like repetition, free association keeps you writing while tricking your logical mind into relinquishing control of a creative process it cannot understand. Begin with the final word of the last sentence you were able to write and let it trigger another word — whatever leaps to mind, however silly. From "silly," the final word of my last sentence, I free-associate *billy…club…rub…rub-a-dub-dub…three men in a tub…bathtub…shower…flower power…hour…time…rhyme…mime…*and on and on. Let each word trigger the next, the next and so on. Relax into it, have fun with it and your flow will return. Again, delete what doesn't belong when you get to your next draft.

3. Talk Jabberwock

"Jabberwocky," if you recall your *Alice in Wonderland,* is the nonsense poem that Alice discovers *Through the Looking Glass.*

> *'Twas brillig, and the slithy toves*
> *Did gyre and gimble in the wabe;*
> *All mimsy were the borogoves,*
> *And the mome raths outgrabe*

When you feel stuck, a little jabberwocking of your own can get you going again. Make up your own words…words that sound funny…words that sound weird…words that don't exist in any known dictionary (like "jabberwock" as a verb). Make one up, write it down…then another…then another…then another. This playful act tricks your inner censor into dropping its guard. Soon, nonsense words will become Muse-sense words and your flow will resume. As with the previous tips, it's about writing *anything* to silence your frightened or hypercritical self and keep the flow alive.

4. Go Foreign

Is English not your first language? Are you fluent enough in a second language to switch linguistic gears for a while? Give it a try. Just remember that whatever the language and whether it's real or made up, the key is to keep writing without stopping. Any way you can do that will help restore the natural free-flow of your Muse Stream.

5. Breathe

If you are stuck in your writing, you are likely stuck in your breath. Are you holding your breath? Has your breathing become shallow? Are you hyperventilating? Focus your awareness on your breath, inhale deeply, hold it for a few counts, then let it go. All of it. Do it again. This time, write "I am breathing in" as you inhale and "I am breathing out" as you exhale. Continue writing your breath until you relax back into the flow.

6. Write Blind

Close your eyes, breathe deeply and write without watching your hand(s), screen or notepad. Removing your attention from the external act of writing and placing it on your breath will carry you inward, away from the source of your anxiety and toward the source of your words and book. Remember to breathe, remember to turn your page if you're writing longhand and remember to keep feeling for the *F* and *J* notches if you're using a traditional keyboard.

Caveat: Proceed with caution. It's easy when writing longhand to write over what you have already written and when on the computer or tablet to hit wrong keys when typing. If auto-save is not enabled on your device, it's equally easy to hit the wrong key sequences when saving manually. I've done all these. I was so in the flow once that I forgot to turn the page and kept writing on top of what I had already written. On the computer, I accidentally erased an entire document because instead of saving, I deleted. There was also one writing session where I typed several pages in a fortunately decipherable "code," when one hand strayed a single key to the right.

7. Get Out of Your Rut

Are you writing on your computer or tablet? Try writing longhand. Are you writing longhand? Exchange your stodgy, blue- or black-ink pen for something colorful, playful, childlike. How about colored pencils or markers? Or crayons? How about different paper? Or turn your page sideways or upside down. Or write in a spiral or around the edges of the paper. Or try doodling through your stuckness. Once again, do anything to keep that pen moving.

8. Change Venues

Where do you normally write? If it's at a desk in your office or study, move into the living room or dining room...or out of the house altogether.

How about a park bench or cafe table? How about setting yourself in front of an inspiring piece of art at a gallery or museum? Or in front of the monkey enclosure at the zoo? Or write in transit — on a random, open-ended bus or subway ride.

9. Move On

Move on to another part of the book, be it to another part of the section that's giving you trouble or to another section altogether. Return to this one in an hour, in a day or in a few days — whenever you feel ready or after you have carried out the necessary research, if a research-deficit is what has stopped you. If you have stopped because this part of the book is emotionally challenging, perhaps it's time to...

10. Explore

Journal on the Muse Stream to explore why you feel stuck. Let whatever emerges guide you back to your manuscript and back into the flow.

Have none of these techniques worked for you? Is your flow still dammed up? Sometimes, the best thing to do to re-prime a gummed-up creative pump is walk away. Perhaps you need to walk away for ten minutes. Perhaps you need to walk away for the rest of the day.

Or perhaps it's time do something unrelated to your book. If researchers at Stanford University are right, your best bet might be to go for a stroll. A recent study found that walking for just eight minutes can substantially boost creativity and that your ability to generate creative ideas continues after the walk is over. You might prefer a nature walk, but their study found no measurable difference between pacing around a drab office or ambling around a leafy campus.

No energy for walking? Take a bath or shower. Read a book for pleasure. Read an author who inspires you. Turn to Section 11 and read "You Are a Writer" or, better yet, get *The Voice of the Muse Companion* CD or MP3, or look up the YouTube video version, and listen to it, repeatedly.

Do you have other creative pursuits? Leave writing behind for a few hours and engage in a different Muse-like pastime: drawing, photography, singing, furniture-making, gardening, cooking — whatever will keep you in a different kind of creative flow until the time is right to return to your book.

Write with Ease on the Muse Stream: A Meditative Experience

This is not only a simple introduction to writing on the Muse Stream, it's a powerful warm-up exercise you can do anywhere, any time.

Set a timer for twenty minutes. Find a comfortable place and position, either by your computer or tablet or with pen and paper by your side.

Close your eyes and take a few deep breaths. As you relax into your breath, feel the stress of your day melt away. Let your shoulders drop, and let all the weight of responsibility and obligation we all often feel melt away on your breath.

Now, let a word or phrase float up into your conscious awareness. Any word or phrase will do.

Once you have your word or words, open your eyes and begin to write, using that word or phrase as your starting point.

Continue writing until the timer goes off, longer if you feel like it. Remember, though, to not stop for any reason. If you feel yourself losing momentum, return to "Help! I'm Stuck!" in the previous chapter.

Remember, this is not about a perfect finished draft. This is about diving into the Muse Stream and discovering how effortless creative flow can be.

Meet Your Muse: A Guided Meditation

ALLOW AT LEAST 30 MINUTES FOR THIS MEDITATION
AND FOR THE WRITING EXPERIENCE THAT FLOWS FROM IT.

Relax. Close your eyes. Get into a comfortable position. Let your shoulders drop. And drop some more.

Take a few deep breaths, breathing in calm and quiet, breathing out fears, fatigue, stress. You're relaxed but alert. Awake and aware. Moving into a quiet place. A deep place. A place of creative freedom, creative vision, creative awakening.

In your mind's eye, see a door. A beautifully crafted door. Handcrafted. A work of art.

Perhaps it's a new door, newly discovered. Perhaps it's ancient, as old as time, just waiting for you to rediscover it. See it or sense it…however you see it or sense it.

This is your doorway of inner vision. Walk up to it. Run your hand over it. Feel its texture…its richness…its depth.

As you touch the door, it swings open. The door to your inner vision will always open at your touch…if you let it.

You are the key.

Now the door swings open and you step across the threshold. Into a wondrous place.

Perhaps you recognize this place. Perhaps it's new. Whatever you see or sense and however you see or sense it is perfect, perfect for you, in this moment.

See or sense this place, this wondrous place. See or sense it fully, using all your senses.

What does it look like? What colors do you see? How is the light? Do you hear any sounds? Smell any smells?

Reach out and touch something. Feel its texture.

What is the spirit of this place? What does it feel like, to you?

Now, coming toward you through this wondrous place, coming toward you bathed in light, is your Muse. Your creative spirit. The being that, in this moment, embodies your purest creative source, that font of creative energy, inspiration and revelation that we all have within us.

This is yours. Unique to you.

However it manifests, whatever you see, sense or feel of it, is right for you. In this moment.

Open your mind and heart. Allow it to come to you in whatever form it comes, recognizing that its form can change from moment to moment, mood to mood, book to book.

There is no right or wrong image, right or wrong way. There is only the way you see or sense, and what you see and sense. And it's perfect. For you.

What does your Muse look like? Feel like to you?

See or sense it fully. Again, use all your physical senses — sight, touch, smell, taste, sound. And your intuitive senses — feeling, spirit, essence.

Your Muse now stands before you, and you greet each other in whatever way feels right, taking all the time you need.

Now, you and your Muse begin a special dialogue.

Perhaps your Muse has a message for you. Perhaps you have questions for your Muse — questions about your book, questions about which is the right book for you right now, questions about your book's theme, content, purpose or vision, or general questions about your creative life.

Be open to whatever comes up. Let the dialogue go where it will.

Take thirty seconds of silence for this conversation. Transcribe it if that will assist you. If you choose to write at this time, pause the recording until you're done.

Now that you feel complete with that interaction, step forward. Take another step. Then another, moving closer and closer to your Muse...until you step into your Muse, until you and your Muse become one, merging in a wondrous moment of creative union.

What does that feel like? What sensations or emotions run through you? What do you see? Sense? Hear? Intuit?

Breathe deeply into the merged entity you are and experience all there is to experience...feel all there is to feel...be all there is to be.

Take twenty seconds of clock time to experience this fully.

Now that you feel complete, step back and away from your Muse. Note any feelings or sensations that action sparks for you. As you step away, thank your Muse for assisting you today and allow your Muse to respond.

Before you leave this place, your Muse hands you a gift, an expression of appreciation for having been freed into your life more consciously. What is it?

Receive this gift and keep it with you. Recall it, if you choose, every time you sit down to work on your book.

Now, turn back to the door — that special door — knowing that you can return to this place at any time to meet with your Muse. All you need to do is remember how it felt to be here. All it takes is stillness. A quiet time. A quiet place, where you're free to envision, where it's safe to create.

Once more, you touch the door, it swings open and you step through… and back.

As you return to your starting place, you bring back with you all that you sensed and all that you saw and all that you heard, felt and intuited. You are bringing it back to your conscious awareness, remembering whatever, in this moment, it serves you to remember.

When you're ready, but only then, open your eyes, staying with all you experienced.

Write about it — what you saw, felt or sensed. What you learned. What you discovered. Write about the conversation you had with your Muse. Write whatever you remember, whatever comes up, taking all the time you need.

Remember to keep your pen moving across the page. Remember to breathe. Remember to censor nothing, freeing the voice of your Muse to live again through you on the page.

- *A version of my recording of this meditation is included — along with ten other, equally inspiring tracks — on "The Voice of the Muse Companion: Guided Meditations for Writers." Look for it on Amazon, iTunes and Google Play and from other online music sellers.*

3. Conception

If it holds no truth, then it cannot truly be story.
MADELEINE L'ENGLE, NOVELIST

*If there's a book you really want to read,
but it hasn't been written yet, then you must write it.*
TONI MORRISON, NOVELIST

Pre-Conception

Your book exists. I know it's hard to believe when all you see in front of you is a blank page or an empty screen. I know it's hard to believe when you gaze down at your virginal white sheet or stare at the pixel blinking at you accusingly and nothing is there — no words, no ideas…no book. I know it's hard to believe when no hint presents itself of which key to press to get started, of which letter to form to launch your book's journey from conception to creation.

The emptiness terrifies you. Of course, it does. "You're not a writer," it shrieks. "If you were, you would know how to start."

Your doubts deepen. "How can there be a book inside me? Why can't I see it? Why can't I know it? Is it even real?"

Your book is real. It's as real as you are. Believe in it as it believes in you. Be ready for it, for it has long been ready for you.

How?

Learn to listen for your book. Learn to listen to your book. It will materialize…as first one word, then another; as first one sentence, then another; as first one page, then another. Then another.

It will materialize if you let it, if you let its words spill out of you, if you let its words continue to spill out of you until the book is written.

It will materialize if you let it.

Let it.

Revelations

I never know what my books will be about when I start writing them. All I know as I begin to write is that I am writing. All I know is that if I allow one word to follow the next and the next and the next, something will emerge — something wiser, more engaging, more illuminating and more creative than anything my conscious mind could have conjured up.

It might be a book. It might not be. It doesn't matter. All that matters is that I answer when my Muse calls. All that matters is that I am writing whatever it is that I am writing.

With three of my books, I didn't even realize I was writing a book.

I birthed my first, *The MoonQuest*, while facilitating a writing workshop in Toronto. Although I rarely write when I'm teaching, an inner voice (my Muse?) insisted that I make an exception. The scene that emerged that evening would become the opening of the first draft of a novel I knew nothing about. (See "Birth of a Book," later in this section.)

If the unexpected fantasy that was *The MoonQuest* quickly identified itself as a book (even as it kept its plot to itself), *The Voice of the Muse: Answering the Call to Write* didn't even bother to tell me that.

It was a few years later and, with *The MoonQuest*'s early drafts completed, I was limping through the first draft of the sequel that would become *The StarQuest*. When the words wouldn't come, which was often, I found myself penning reams of self-motivating vignettes, writings that would later form the foundation of *The Voice of the Muse*.

In unwittingly writing *The Voice of the Muse*, I was using something I call "meditative dialogue" (see "Talk to Your Book" in Section 5), a tool I then often used when feeling troubled and one I had used to great effect a few years earlier during an emotionally charged five-month retreat. Those meditative dialogues, also originally written only for me, would become *Dialogues with the Divine*, another book that wrote itself without me realizing what I was doing.

Of course, not all my books have emerged that way. But even when I know something of a book's theme or subject, I rarely start with more than a title or with the vaguest hint of an idea. I just start and let the book reveal itself to me in the writing of it. That was true of *The StarQuest* and *The SunQuest*. It was true of my *Acts of Surrender* memoir. It has been true of each of my books for writers, including this one. It has been equally true for my screenplays, stage plays, essays, blog posts and occasional poetical dabblings.

Some of those writing projects played out as I expected. Most did not. And all veered in unanticipated directions that, without exception, produced a more compelling result.

In the end, each book shaped itself — not to what I thought it should be, but to what it knew itself to be. My job was to get out its way and let it.

How did I do that? By writing on the Muse Stream, by setting pen to paper or fingers to keyboard, allowing the river of words to flow on their own undirected course and trusting the voyage of discovery inherent in all creative life.

Whatever you know of your book and its content, you start every piece of writing the same way, with a single word. With a single letter. With a single pen stroke or key stroke.

Any word. Any letter. Any pen stroke or tap on the keyboard. It doesn't matter which because however you begin, your beginning is but the inauguration of a journey into the unknown that will repeatedly spiral you back to your starting point, each return relaunching you from a place of ever-increasing creative wisdom and insight.

Do you know what your book is about? If you don't, the Muse Stream will soon reveal it to you. If you do, that same free-flowing stream will get it onto the page for you — naturally, spontaneously and without struggle.

Either way, the Muse Stream is waiting to help you birth and complete your book. All you have to do is let it.

- *Experience the same writing exercise that birthed* The MoonQuest *in* "Birthing Your Book: A Meditative Journey," *later in this section.*

The Soul of Your Book

You assume that creation is about bringing something into the world out of nothing or, at best, out of some raw material like clay or wood. Creation is more than that. In creating, you are not fashioning something out of nothing.

When a new being is created from the loving union of a man and woman, has that being been created out of nothing? No. That being's spirit and soul were already present. But it took the blending of two beings and the raw materials of sperm and egg to set in motion the miracle that would unite a soul with its newly forming body.

Your book is no different. Just as the soul of a new human being is eternal and does not need to be created, for it already is, so the book you have set out to write does not need to be created, at least not in the "manufacturing" sense we commonly associate with the word "create."

The soul of your book already exists, and within that soul is encoded its words and form. As you connect with that soul by writing on the Muse Stream or through whatever connecting practice you use, your book's words and form will willingly make themselves known to you.

A blank page means only that the page is blank. It does not mean that the book you seek to create isn't already present within it. It is — in its completeness and in its perfection.

That you cannot yet see it does not negate its existence. Rather, it confirms the current limits of your vision.

Throw off your blinders, open your heart and begin to see past the apparent emptiness of your page and into the soul of your book, into the true soul of creation.

No, you are not creating something from nothing as you write this book. You are emptying yourself of all preconceptions save the true *pre*conception: the energy before conception that waits to be heard.

Listen for that energy. Listen to that energy. And free into form that which is already present in the infinite. Free it into your heart. Free it onto the page. Free it to become the book you have come here to write.

Try This

As you sit down to write today, commit to abandoning all preconceptions and surrendering to *pre*-conception. Say aloud: "As the author I am, I allow this book to emerge into its natural form and flow into its idea of perfection, not mine. I surrender to the book and let it flow."

Now, let it flow.

Your Ocean of Stories

You carry an ocean of stories within you, an infinite wellspring of knowledge and wisdom, of exploits, experiences and emotions, which sometimes only surface to conscious awareness in the writing of them.

Like the mightiest of the earth's seas, your storied sea is a place of magic and mystery, danger and delight…a medley of the known and the unexplored, a blend of the murky and the magnificent.

You dive into that ocean when you embark on a book-writing journey. And like all the great explorers who have preceded you, you may think you know what you will find on your odyssey. Even as you will surely encounter the expected, this journey into your ocean of stories will often astound you as it reveals treasures long ago forgotten. It will occasionally alarm you as it reveals emotions long ago buried.

Don't let your ocean's uncharted depths frighten you into abandoning the adventure. Dive in. Dive into the words. Dive into the stories. Dive into the ocean of your book.

You will not disappear into that ocean. You will not drown in its waves. Its waters will support you. Its waters will baptize and anoint you. And you will emerge from those sacred waters transformed in ways you cannot now imagine.

It's impossible to control the changes that will have their way with you through this ocean crossing, just as it's impossible to control the words that pass onto the page as you write on the Muse Stream. But in immersing yourself in your sea of stories, you *will* be changed.

Why? The act of writing a book, of converting wisdom to words on a page, is a revolutionary one. Whatever your book, you must be open to the possibility of inner revolution, without knowing what it will look like or how it will resolve itself — in your book any more than in your life.

All you can do is recognize the truth of this moment, of this feeling, of this book, of this word…and move on to the next from a place of trust.

Trust your book, and yourself — through each word and sentence — until your page is alive with the wonder of creation, until you are in awe at the life of your creation…and at the creation of your life.

Your Ocean of Stories: A Guided Meditation

ALLOW AT LEAST 30 MINUTES FOR THIS MEDITATION
AND FOR THE WRITING EXPERIENCE THAT FLOWS FROM IT.

Relax. Allow your breath to slow and deepen, slow and deepen, slow and deepen.

Close your eyes for a moment and picture an ocean. Any ocean. Anywhere. An ocean you have seen or visited, or one that resides only in your heart.

Whichever it is, see that ocean stretching out to the horizon, seemingly limitless in its scope. Feel its infinite nature, its infinite depth, its infinite breadth. Know that every book you have ever written or will write resides in that ocean, just as that ocean resides within you. Know that every book you have ever written or will write is as real and alive now as the sea life that thrives deep below the ocean surface of your imagining.

See yourself now in a boat on that ocean. Open ocean. A large boat or small. It doesn't matter as long as you feel safe, as long as you're comfortable, as long as it's your boat. Get a sense of that boat that now carries you, supports you, propels you forward. Feel the salt spray on your face. Feel the gentle swell of the ocean's ebb and flow.

Ebb and flow.

Ebb and flow.

Allow your breathing to align with that ebb and flow as you become one with this environment you are creating. This ocean. This boat. This sea of stories that stretches as far as the eye can see.

Farther.

If your boat is moving, allow it now to slow or stop. Anywhere. Anywhere at all. As long as you remain in open waters. Drop anchor or allow yourself to drift. It doesn't matter.

Now, in your hands is a net, a special net that scoops up not fish but books and the stories that fill them. Books and stories from the vast undersea world that is the infinite reservoir of your imagination, experience and creativity.

Take a deep breath now and cast your net into this sea of your creativity. Cast your net and let it fall where it falls, sinking wherever it sinks.

Take a few more breaths, allowing your net to settle. As your net sinks and settles, take a few more breaths, in and out, your breath following the ocean's swell. In and out. In and out. In and out.

Now it's time to raise your net. So do it. Raise your net and see what you have retrieved. What you have received.

Whatever it is is perfect. Perhaps what has emerged makes sense as a book. Perhaps it makes no sense to your conscious mind. It doesn't matter. Whatever it is is perfect in this moment. For this moment.

What have you retrieved from the ocean of story? From the depths of your creative waters?

See it. Feel it. Sense it. Know it. Fully.

Now, write it.

- *A version of my recording of this meditation is included — along with ten other, equally inspiring tracks — on "The Voice of the Muse Companion: Guided Meditations for Writers." Look for it on Amazon, iTunes and Google Play and from other online music sellers.*

In the Beginning Was the Word

"In the beginning was the Word," the Gospels proclaim. They then go on to remind us that "the Word was with God."

The first word of your book also resides with God…or your Muse…or the sentient essence of your book…or whatever creative source you acknowledge. So does your second and third word and your thirtieth and thirty-thousandth.

Whichever word gets you started is the right one. And that right one will inexorably lead you to the next and the next and the next. And the next. If you let it.

Ultimately, all those words will lead you through your book to its ending, an ending that has been waiting for you since the beginning of time. Of course it has, for your book has existed since the beginning of time, waiting patiently for you acknowledge it, open your heart to it and capture its essence in words on a page.

Are you ready to acknowledge it? Then pick up your pen or touch your fingers to the keyboard and free your first word onto the page. Let that one word lead to a second and a third, trusting that the words that emerge are precisely the ones that will move your book forward

You still don't know what your book is about? If you listen it will tell you. If you surrender, it will guide you. If you let it, it will write itself.

Try This

Pick a word, any word. Let it be the first random word that comes to mind or the first word your eyes light on as you glance around the room. Or flip to a page in this or any book, close your eyes and let your finger blindly search out the word that will launch your day's writing…that may launch your book.

Don't second-guess the word that emerges. Don't discard your word and try again if you don't like what your mind or finger has come up with. Don't dismiss even the most unexceptional of words, even something as innocuous as "a" or "the" or "of" or "and" or "but." Your book, in its wisdom, chose this word. Your job is to surrender to it.

Now, take a few deep breaths into your word.

Embody that word.

Fill yourself with that word and fill that word with all of you.

Write the word.

Without stopping to think about it, let another word follow that one. And another. And another.

What about sentences and paragraphs? What about a subject?

You are the subject. I don't mean you will be writing about yourself — although at some unconscious level you always are. What I mean here is that you are the subject and your pen is sovereign. If you let it, that pen will carry you on an extraordinary journey of discovery. If you let go and surrender to the journey, you will find yourself writing flowingly and freely, letting the sentences of your book unfold without your conscious mind getting in the way.

Continue to write on the Muse Stream for at least 20 minutes; make it 30 or 45, if you can…60, if you dare.

Remember to write without stopping, to write without editing or correcting, to write without thinking or censoring. To go with first thoughts. To write without judging. Write until you feel complete. Then write for 10 minutes more.

Explorations

Ask yourself these questions and don't think about the answers. Let them emerge freely and honestly…on the Muse Stream, where appropriate:
- Was it easy for me to stay in the flow? Or was I tempted to edit, censor or second-guess?
- What did I discover from my writing? About my book? About myself? About my creative process?
- Did continuing for those additional 10 minutes reveal something unexpected? About me? About my book? About my creative process?

Keys to Your Kingdom of Creation

If you aren't sure what your book is about or where to begin, if you have already begun and find yourself stuck, or if you need a quick exercise to get you going, pick a writing prompt from "Fifty Keys to Your Book's Conception and Creation," below, using any of the following methods:
- Pick a word at random.
- Close your eyes and let your finger drop to a word or phrase.
- Close your eyes, choose a number between one and fifty, then let that number direct you to your key.
- Run through the list in order.

As with all exercises in *Birthing Your Book*, have fun with the list and feel free to adapt it to your needs and your book's: Alter words or phrases, combine words or phrases, turn positive statements into negatives or change genders and tenses.

Alternatively, use the exercise that follows the list to come up with a key word or phrase of your own.

Remember to write on the Muse Stream — without thinking, judging or censoring. Simply let your book's words fall naturally onto the page.

Don't worry how, where or whether what you write will fit into your book. Some of it will and some of it won't. Your job is not to figure anything out. Your job is to write.

By the way, I call these writing prompts "key" words or phrases because the word or phrase that launches your writing journey is the key that undams your Muse Stream and unlocks the natural free-flow of your creativity...and your book.

Fifty Keys to Your Book's Conception and Creation

1. In the beginning...
2. Red.
3. If I could...
4. My book is...
5. I wish...

6. She regretted…
7. The body…
8. You don't understand!
9. I wish I had written…
10. Once upon a time…
11. Murder.
12. Before I die…
13. He cheated…
14. "I don't want to interrupt—"
15. Escape…
16. Love isn't…
17. His/her biggest secret is…
18. When the curtain opened…
19. "Hide!"
20. I write because…
21. God.
22. Words.
23. Twice upon a time…
24. Where?
25. By the end of this book, I want…
26. "Perhaps not."
27. If this book were fiction/nonfiction/a poem/a movie…
28. I want people to say about my book that…
29. I dream…
30. To be or not to be…
31. Sexy.
32. Just try and stop me!
33. The G-man and the G-string…
34. Good, better, best…
35. Don't touch me!
36. The money was…
37. Red rover…

38. The bicycle...
39. Celine Dion [or your favorite/least favorite celebrity] will love my book because...
40. "Get out of my bed!"
41. The eagle feather...
42. Making love.
43. Hate.
44. They don't trust...
45. I can't find it!
46. The music the wind makes is...
47. The sound of the tree bark was...
48. The end.
49. The beginning.
50. A new beginning.

TRY THIS

There are many creative ways to arrive at your own key word or phrase. Here's a workshop favorite that often produces surprisingly profound results. All you need is a blank sheet of unlined paper, a couple of colored pencils, markers or crayons and, of course, writing paper.

Holding one or two of the markers in one hand, close your eyes and, without peeking, begin to draw, doodle or make whatever markings you feel called to make. Keep at it for 20 to 30 seconds, without lifting your pen(s) from the page.

When it's time to open your eyes, breathe deeply and, without judgment, look at your drawing without trying to analyze it. Continue to focus on your breath and let one, two or three words or phrases bubble up into consciousness, triggered by your drawing. Don't judge or censor what emerges, no matter what it is.

As these words or phrases come to you, jot them down next to your drawing with one of your markers.

Using the word or phrase that has the most power for you, begin to write on the Muse Stream — with a colored marker if you prefer. Write for 10, 20 or 30 minutes. If you had more than one key word or phrase, write again using the next most powerful word or phrase.

Remember to always keep your pen moving. If you can't, revisit "Help! I'm Stuck!" in Section 2.

Birth of a Book

It's March 1994. I see *The Celtic Tarot* divination deck in Toronto's Omega Centre bookstore and it so seduces me that I can't walk away from it, even though I don't know how to read tarot and have no desire to learn. What I am learning is to trust my intuition, so after several attempts to leave the store empty-handed, I finally surrender, despite the deck's discomfiting price tag.

A few mornings later, I'm preparing for a writing workshop I am to teach when *The Celtic Tarot* catches my eye from across the room. As I thumb through the deck with its evocative major arcana cards, I realize why I had to have it: I will use it as part of a writing exercise for the workshop.

That evening, I have each student draw, closed-eyed, one of the major arcana cards. I then have them open their eyes as I guide them through a meditative journey into writing.

Everyone immediately launches into a frenzy of creative output and I'm relieved, not only because the exercise is working but because it has justified my extravagant purchase.

I rarely write during a workshop that I'm facilitating. Instead, I keep an eye on participants in case anyone needs help. This class is different. Within moments, some inner imperative insists that I also draw a card. I reach into the deck and pull out The Chariot.

Without full awareness of what I'm doing, I pick up my pen, pull my yellow-paged notepad toward me and begin to write. What emerges, after a rambling preamble, is the tale of an odd-looking man in an odd-looking coach. Pulling the coach are horses as oddly colored as those on the Chariot card.

I know nothing about this man and his horses. I know nothing about this story. All I know is what emerges, word by word, onto the page.

Next morning, lured back into the story, I add to it. I continue adding to it daily, almost obsessively, rarely knowing from one day to the next what the story is about or where it is carrying me. A year later on the anniversary of that Toronto class, I complete my first draft of the fantasy novel that has become *The MoonQuest*.

It's May 2007, 2,800 miles away and many drafts and years later. I open my email to a JPEG from Courtney Davis, the British artist who created *The Celtic Tarot*. The image is The Chariot card, which I haven't seen since I gave my copy of the deck to a tarot-reader friend in 1997. Davis has sent the JPEG to tweak my memory so that I can write a caption for it, for an upcoming retrospective of his art.

When I see The Chariot for the first time in a decade, I'm startled. Even though the artist who designed *The MoonQuest*'s first-edition cover never saw the tarot card and knows nothing of *The Celtic Tarot* or how it inspired me, there is a marked similarity between the two. Not only are the horses identically colored, they are identically placed. There is even a tiny chalice tucked above the wording on the card.

Although I have retired that original cover, The Chariot's inspiration is still evident throughout *The MoonQuest* — a story that knew itself far better than I did…a story that knew me better than I knew myself…a story that insisted I trust it to reveal itself to me, moment by moment, word by word…a story that has never let me down.

Explorations

Ask yourself these questions and don't think about the answers. Let them emerge freely and honestly…on the Muse Stream, where appropriate:
- How can I trust my book to reveal itself to me?
- How can I surrender more fully to the mystery of the blank page?
- Can I write the book that wants to be written by me, even if I don't yet know what it is?
- Can I start? Now?

Birthing Your Book: A Meditative Journey

ALLOW AT LEAST 40 MINUTES FOR THIS MEDITATIVE EXERCISE
AND FOR THE WRITING EXPERIENCE THAT FLOWS FROM IT.

This is a version of the meditative exercise that birthed *The MoonQuest*. For it, you will need a selection of evocative images, preferably ones toward which you have no conscious emotional connection. For example:
- Any divination or oracle deck, including a tarot deck. (If it's a tarot deck where the minor arcana comprise only numbers, as was the case with *The Celtic Tarot*[1], separate out the major arcana cards and use only those.)
- Photos or graphics clipped from a magazine or printed out from the Internet.
- A coffee table book of photography or art reproductions.
- A writing colleague's family photo album or travel pics.
- A stranger's Instagram, Flickr or other photo feed.

If you are working on a memoir, autobiography, biography or history, use old photos that relate to you or to your subject.

Alternatively, take yourself off to a museum, art gallery or sculpture garden and park yourself on a bench with a good view of several works of art. Then, adapt the following exercise to your location.

Find a quiet place where you will not be disturbed, and get comfortable. This is an exercise designed to get you writing, so have pen and paper, tablet or computer within easy reach.

Close your eyes, take a few deep breaths, in and out, and relax. Breathe in to your creative source, whatever that is for you, and breathe out all doubt, fear and judgment.

Place your palm against your heart and breathe in to your heart, then breathe out everything that is not heart.

Let your breath wash away all anxiety, stress or strain. Let it wash away all feelings that you must control this experience.

---

[1] Unfortunately, the Courtney Davis *Celtic Tarot* that birthed *The MoonQuest* is now out-of-print, although used and collectable editions can still be found online.

Breathe in deeply, and let yourself surrender fully to this moment…and now this one.

Continue to focus on your breath and, remaining in a meditative space, open your eyes.

If you are working with loose images (photos, etc.), shuffle them at least three times, keeping them face down. When you feel ready, pick a card or photo but don't look at it yet.

If you are working with a book or album, open it at random, bookmarking the selected page with your finger. But don't open the book to look at the image.

If you are working with an Instagram or other photo feed, keep your eyes closed as you use your finger (phone/tablet) or mouse (computer) to blindly scroll up and down the screen to select an image. Turn away from the device so as not to see what you chose.

Close your eyes again for a few moments and, once again, return your focus to your breath. Breath in and out a few more times, as deeply as you are able to.

Now, focus your breath on the image you have chosen, the image you have not yet seen. Breathe in to it. Feel yourself connect with it. Become one with it, whatever it is.

Remaining in that meditative space, gently open your eyes. Continue to focus on your breath as you breathe into your image and either turn over your chosen card or picture or open your book or album to the page you have bookmarked.

Before looking at your image closely, I would like you to just take it in. The whole image. An overview. As though you are gazing down on a landscape that is miles below you, as though you are looking down from an alpine summit or from an airplane window. Ignore the details for now. Take it in. Breathe it in.

Ask yourself these questions, now and throughout your experience with this image, and censor nothing:

- How does the image make you feel?
- What emotions does it evoke?
- What physical sensations does it arouse?
- Does it trigger any thoughts or memories? Any associations? Anything else?
- Does it make you uncomfortable in any way? How?
- Alternatively, is it comforting or reassuring in some way? How?

Now, still ignoring its specifics, take in the colors, hues, shadows and shadings of the image. Its shapes. Its areas of brightness. Its areas of dark. And everything in between.

Remember to keep breathing, deeply.

What do you feel now?
And now?

Now it's time to zoom in to the specifics of the image, to its details. What is your first thought as you look at this image more closely?

Look at it more closely still. Notice details that you might have missed previously. Let your eyes slowly spiral into the center of the image, starting at the lower left corner and continuing counterclockwise until you get to the center.

Rest for a few breaths at the center of the image and then return, in a clockwise direction, back to the outer edges.

As you travel the image in this way, be aware of what you notice and feel.

When you have completed your two circuits, back up to a middle view of the image.

Whether the image is realistic or abstract, imagine it in motion. What does that look like? What story does it tell?

Now, step inside the image. Step inside it and engage with it in whatever way feels right. As you do, bring all your senses into play.

Don't judge or second-guess. Simply experience what you experience, and surrender into it.

- What do things look like from the inside? In what ways are they different than they were from the outside?
- What do you see beyond the frame of your image that is invisible from the outside?
- What smells do you smell?
- What can you reach out and touch? What does it feel like?
- What can you taste or imagine tasting?
- What do you hear?
- Is there anyone (or anything) you can interact with? If so, do it.

Surrender fully into this part of the exercise and give yourself all the time you need for it. When you are complete, continue on to the final portion.

Now, step back outside the image, return to where you were at the start of the exercise and take one last look into your card, photo or art piece. Notice anything you might have missed before. Note any emotions or associations you didn't feel earlier. Be aware of any new physical sensations.

If you already know what you feel called to write from the experience, go ahead and start. If you are unsure, let one of your impressions or experiences of the image be the key that unlocks your creative journey. Alternatively, use the key phrase, "This picture is…" or "This picture says…" or "This picture could be…"

Remember to write on the Muse Stream, without stopping. If you get stuck, keep your pen moving — through repetition, free association or nonsense words or by describing the image. Remember, too, to be aware of your breath.

As you write, ignore all concerns about spelling, punctuation or grammar. Don't worry if what you are writing seems to make no sense or seems to have nothing to do with your book. Start, and let the writing carry you where it will — into a new book, deeper into an existing one or on a journey whose aim and destination will make themselves known to you in their own way and in their own time.

4. Mark David's "Rules" for Birthing Your Book

Without freedom there can be no creativity.
JUDITH WESTON, AUTHOR

*The man who writes about himself and his own time
is the only man who writes about all people and about all time.*
GEORGE BERNARD SHAW, PLAYWRIGHT

Twenty Rules for Birthing Your Book

Follow these twenty so-called "rules" and you will never again struggle in your book-birthing, or in any other of your creative expressions or endeavors. Of course, given Rule #1, it's up to you to make these rules your own and to adapt them to your particular needs and projects. (I explore each rule in more depth in the chapters that follow.)

RULE #1
There are no rules.

RULE #2
Be in the moment.

RULE #3
You don't have to know what your book is about
before you start writing.

RULE #4
Surrender to the Muse Stream.

RULE #5
Lose your mind and follow your heart.

RULE #6
Take risks.

RULE #7
Be vulnerable.

RULE #8
Your book is boss.

RULE #9
Your book is a trickster.

Rule #10
Embrace the chaos.

Rule #11
It's all in order…even if it's not.

Rule #12
Your book is perfect…even if it's not.

Rule #13
Practice discernment.

Rule #14
Write *your* right book.

Rule #15
Write what's right for you right now.

Rule #16
Market trends are irrelevant.

Rule #17
Write!

Rule #18
Set yourself up for success.

Rule #19
Commit to yourself as the writer you are.

Rule #20
There are no rules!

Rule #1: There Are No Rules

I have many rules that are not rules at all, among them rules for writing your screenplay, rules for writing your memoir, general rules for writing, rules for revision (Section 8) and rules for living a creative life (Section 10). Regardless of its theme or thrust, each set begins and ends the same way:

Rule #1
There Are No Rules

That's right. No rules. At least none that matter.

The realm of the imagination can be subject to no laws, no statutes, no proclamations. It bows down to neither commandments nor edicts. The realm of the imagination is sovereign.

The landscape of the imagination has no predetermined roads, paths or trails, nor has it any maps. The landscape of the imagination is uncharted.

In this kingdom, you are explorer and trailblazer. In this kingdom, there is no one right way or wrong way to conceive, craft and complete your book, whatever it's about.

Whatever it's about, it's your book, the singular creation of your unique heart and art. No one else can write your book, hence no one else's rules can govern it.

The only rule is that there are no rules and the only right way is the way that works for you, in the moment. So *be* in the moment with your book, which just happens to be Rule #2.

But before we get there…

Explorations

Ask yourself these questions and don't think about the answers. Let them emerge freely and honestly…on the Muse Stream, where appropriate:

- Where in my writing am I letting other people's rules, paths and ways of doing things get in the way of discovering my own? What about in my life?
- Where am I a follower when I could be an explorer and trailblazer? How can I make that shift? With this book I'm writing? With my writing in general? In my life?

- Where am I being ruled by others' expectations for me? For my writing? For my book? In my life?
- Where is my discernment being overruled by my fear?
- What can I do, starting today, to better chart my own course with my book? With my writing? In my life?
- Which "rule" have I been following that I can break today? Right now?

The Power of Now

There is never any need to think ahead to your next word, sentence, paragraph or chapter...or book. Like your next breath, your next word will always come if you get out of its way and let it, if you stay focused on the word of the moment and dissolve all thoughts about the words that have yet to come.

RULE #2
Be in the Moment

Your only responsibility is to the word you are writing right now. I'm not talking about *worry*-responsibility; I'm talking about *surrender*-responsibility. If you surrender to creativity's natural spontaneity without judging, planning or second-guessing, your next word will always drop easily onto the page. Not only that, if you get out of its way and free it to emerge on its own, that next word will be more insightful, engaging and original than anything you could work at, figure out or consciously craft.

TRY THIS

Go for a walk — in nature, around the block, down a busy street or anywhere that offers you some degree of sensory stimulation. As you walk, do your best to stay in the present moment, focusing only on your five senses and on what you see, hear, touch, smell or taste from breath to breath. As your mind wanders, and it will, acknowledge each stimulus, saying (aloud or silently), "I see/smell/hear/touch/taste the..." and repeating the phrase as you walk, as often as you need to keep focused on the now.

Remember this exercise next time you are working on your book and, as your mind moves away from the word of the moment, bring it back — gently and without judgment.

TRY THIS TOO

If you have a meditation practice, treat your writing time as a form of meditation, applying to it all your usual stay-in-the-moment techniques.

Consider priming yourself for this now-moment zone by meditating before you write.

If you don't meditate, use your breath to help keep you focused on the word you are writing, just as you did in "Help! I'm Stuck!" (Section 2).

TRY THIS AS WELL

Look for ways to better demarcate your Muse-centered book-birthing time from the logical, mind-centered universe in which we spend much of our time. Here are some suggestions to help you transition from the mundane into the creative:

- Go for a walk to clear your head. Incorporate the in-the-moment exercise on the previous page if that helps.
- Do yoga or other stretching exercises, or take up tai chi or a similar centering discipline.
- Listen to a relaxation recording or to one of the tracks on *The Voice of the Muse Companion: Guided Meditations for Writers*.
- If you have created a vision statement (see Section 7), read it aloud — slowly and with intention — before you start writing.

AND TRY THIS

Use this quick meditation before you write or to recenter when you find yourself stressed or distracted in the midst of your writing...or at any other time.

Sit down — at your desk, in your favorite chair, in your favorite part of the garden, in your favorite park or on your favorite beach...wherever you feel comfortable, safe and inspired. Close your eyes, place your hands on your empty lap and breathe...in and out slowly, as slowly as you can, for ten breaths.

Breathe more slowly with each breath and feel your body relax. Feel each in-breath connect you to your book, your creative source or your Muse. Feel each out-breath flush all fear, doubt and anxiety from your system, flush all worldly concerns from your mind.

Focus on your heart and breathe into that space, into that fire, into that well of passion and creativity where your book resides. Breathe into the writing you intend to begin or continue. Breathe into the light and life and heart of it. Breathe into your heart connection with it. Breathe into your vision for it. Breathe into your truth.

Breathe in, breathe out and listen. If you find yourself ready to dive onto the blank page or screen before your ten breaths are up, go for it. This is not about rules. This is about getting you primed. Once you're primed, leap onto the page and let the words of your book spill out of you.

Do You Know What Your Book Is About?

Too many books, teachers and writing gurus require you to know what your book is about before you begin. Some even insist that you outline it ahead of time. They haven't heard about my Book-Birthing Rule #3.

Rule #3
You Don't Have to Know What Your Book Is About Before You Start Writing

You don't have to know anything about your book's theme, thrust or plot in order to begin. All you have to do is begin. All you have to do is write one word, then another, then another. Then another, all the way to the end.

As you do that, in surrender to the word of the moment and in surrender to the superior wisdom of your book (see Rule #8), the book you know nothing about will reveal itself to you.

- *Revisit Section 3, "Conception," for more about discovering what your book is about and for tips on getting started.*

"I Don't Know How to Start (or Finish) My Book"

Of course you know how to start. That's what the Muse Stream is for. You don't have a theme, topic or opening? Pick a word, any word, and start. Keep writing without stopping, and don't think.

You don't know how it's going to end? You don't have to. Perhaps it's even better if you don't. Regardless, all you need to know in this moment is the next word. One word. Any word. It doesn't even matter what that word is. If you write on the Muse Stream, if you put your faith in the superior wisdom of your book and abandon all preconceptions, that one word will take you where you need to go. Always.

Your sole/soul responsibility is to begin. So begin.

Your sole/soul responsibility is to continue. So continue.

Drop a word onto a page. Any word. Then another. And another. Follow the words where they take you as they reveal the book you have come here to birth.

Rule #4

Surrender to the Muse Stream

As you move forward, remember that your page is blank for a reason. It's waiting for your creation, for the voice of your Muse to push, cajole, sweet-talk, threaten or charm you into filling it. You will fill it more quickly, easily, naturally and spontaneously if you surrender — to the Muse Stream and to your book.

- *Have you read "Write with Ease on the Muse Stream" yet? If not, bookmark this page and return to Section 2. You can't surrender to the Muse Stream if you don't know what it is!*

Explorations

Ask yourself these questions and don't think about the answers. Let them emerge freely and honestly…on the Muse Stream, where appropriate:

- Am I still stopping to edit as I go?

- Am I still stopping to think? About what to write next? About what I have already written? About what people will think about what I'm writing?
- Have I gone back over what I have already written instead of focusing on the word I am writing? (Remember Rule #2?)
- Am I looking backward instead of continuing to move forward with my book? (See "The Coppola Method," Section 5.)
- Am I giving in to second thoughts and censoring myself?
- Am I letting my doubts and judgments get in the way of the natural free-flow of my creativity?
- Are there other ways in which I am still resisting the Muse Stream?

If you answered yes to any of those questions, redouble your efforts, without being punishing about it, to follow the Muse Stream's basic precepts as you write, feeling free to adapt them to the particular needs of your project *without diluting them*.

Try This

Have you started writing your book yet? If so, put my book down and return to yours, picking up where you left off and writing whatever comes to you to write. If not, it's time to start. It doesn't matter how you start or where you start. All that matters is that you do. In either case, remember to surrender to the Muse Stream.

Forget Everything You Think You Know About Writing

Forget your grade school teacher who was a stickler for spelling, punctuation and grammar. Forget your high school teacher who forced you to turn in an outline with your essay. Forget your college professor who forced you to write to a certain form or style. Forget the writers, classmates and instructors who cruelly critiqued or ridiculed you. Forget every writing manual and book-writing how-to you have ever read (including, where appropriate, this one). Forget everything you think you know about book-writing, and remember this:

Rule #5
Lose Your Mind and Follow Your Heart

Your heart? Yes. Because that's where your book resides, where it has always resided…where it has been waiting for you to acknowledge it so that you can release it onto the page.

Your heart is the smartest brain, strongest muscle, most developed tool in your body. Your heart is your connection to your creativity, to your Muse, to your book.

Your brain isn't that muscle, although without it you couldn't translate that connection into words, sentences, chapters and books. Your brain is not that connecting place. Your heart is.

When you follow your heart and lose your mind, you free yourself of fear, worry and anxiety. When you follow your heart and lose your mind, you silence your second-guessing inner critic. When you follow your heart and lose your mind, you free yourself of all restrictions and constrictions, all expectations and preconceptions, all should's, must's and have-to's.

When you follow your heart and lose your mind, you are never derivative, manipulative, hackneyed, conventional or trite. When you follow your heart and lose your mind, you are creative, innovative and original.

When you follow your heart and lose your mind, you write the book only you can write in the way that only you can write it.

Explorations

Ask yourself these questions and don't think about the answers. Let them emerge freely and honestly…on the Muse Stream, where appropriate:

- In what ways have I been caught up in fear, worry and anxiety in my book-birthing?
- Where have I been letting my mind instead of my heart, intuition and discernment take the lead role in my book-birthing? What concrete steps can I take right now to find a better balance between heart and mind?
- How can I start trusting myself, my Muse and my book more than I have allowed myself to do before now?
- What can I do in my next writing session to let my heart take charge?

Go Boldly

Creative expression is about risk-taking. It's about boarding *Star Trek*'s starship *Enterprise*, taking off for parts unknown and journeying to the edges of the creative universe. It's about boarding your inner-space probe and voyaging to galaxies within yourself that you have never before dared explore.

Rule #6
Take Risks

"You've got to go out on a limb," humorist Will Rogers is reputed to have said, "because that's where the fruit is." The fruit is your originality. The fruit is your ingenuity. The fruit is your inventiveness. The fruit is your *un*conventional wisdom. The fruit is the theme, approach or content that is unique to you, the literary place where no other writer has dared go. The fruit is the "creative" in your creative expression.

That's the good news. The bad news, which isn't so bad, is that when you take risks in your writing, not everyone is going to like your book. Chances are that someone is going to hate your book. It's even possible that someone is going to hate you for having written that book.

It's all right to offend people, to push people's buttons, to take them up to that ledge on which we, as artists, live…and then to give them a gentle nudge. Art is about pushing boundaries — your own as well as those of others. It's about forcing people (including the artist) out of stale comfort zones and inciting them to reexamine their beliefs and rediscover who they think they are. Sometimes, it's about getting people mad at you. Sometimes, it's good to get people mad at you — for them and for you.

Commit today to taking more risks. Commit today to going out on a limb. Commit today to letting yourself be judged…and letting it be okay.

Explorations

Ask yourself these questions and don't think about the answers. Let them emerge freely and honestly…on the Muse Stream, where appropriate:

- Where am I going out on a limb and taking risks with my book?

- Where am I staying on the ground and clinging to the tree trunk to play it safe?
- Where am I willing to challenge established authority and convention?
- Where am I willing to get people riled up?
- Where am I holding myself back for fear of being judged, shamed, ridiculed or attacked?

Try This

Write something, anything, that you consider risky — something that challenges conventional wisdom (including your own)…that pushes buttons (including your own)…that pushes boundaries (including your own). Let it be part of your book if that's possible. If not, do it in your *Birthing Your Book* journal as an exercise in risky writing.

Don't do it just once. Do it regularly. Keep pressing up against the limits of your comfort zone. Keep finding ways to go out on a limb with your writing. Keep taking risks!

The Naked Truth

I was living about two hours north of Toronto on Lake Huron's Georgian Bay in 1997 when a series of Muse Stream-like writings began pushing themselves through me. Two, three, sometimes four times a day during this five-month retreat, an irresistible force would propel me to my journal, where I would release a flood of self-directed inspiration onto the page.

"Walk the earth naked, clothed only in your truth," I wrote early on in the book that would become *Dialogues with the Divine: Encounters with My Wisest Self*. It was a call that would repeat itself often over the next years, never more insistently than while I was working on *Acts of Surrender: A Writer's Memoir*. This injunction, as I write in the memoir, "wasn't about coming out as a gay man. I had done that more than a decade earlier with minimal fallout. It was about coming out as frightened, vulnerable and imperfect. It was about coming out as human."

Rule #7

Be Vulnerable

Your vulnerability will always engage your readers. Often, it will also move them. This is not about being a self-indulgent exhibitionist. It's about expressing yourself from a place of passion and emotion. It's about revealing all of who you are — fears, warts and all — through your writing.

You start by opening your heart to yourself. You continue by letting that openness, honesty and authenticity infuse everything you write, regardless of form, genre or medium.

This is particularly true in memoir or personal essay. It's equally true in fiction and other forms of nonfiction.

In some ways, my *Q'ntana Trilogy* novels and my books for writers reveal more about me than does my memoir. That didn't happen because I consciously exposed my hidden selves in those books. It happened because, with intention, I committed to withholding nothing of who I am that might be relevant to those books. The revelations are less in the lines of the books than between the lines, unconscious byproducts of my willingness to "walk the earth naked" in my writing, to clothe myself only in the truths of my heart.

Explorations

Ask yourself these questions and don't think about the answers. Let them emerge freely and honestly...on the Muse Stream, where appropriate:
- Where in my book am I refusing to reveal myself to my readers?
- Where in my book am I refusing to reveal myself to me?
- Where in my book am I myself holding back from writing from places of powerful emotion, especially those emotions I would rather avoid?
- Where in my book am I holding myself back from walking the earth naked, clothed only in my truth?
- Where in my book am I refusing to be vulnerable and authentic?
- How else am I censoring myself in my book?

Try This

Repeat the risky-writing exercise from Rule #6, only this time make the subject *you*. Whether it's for your book or not, walk the earth naked in your writing and expose your vulnerability to yourself and to the world.

Your Book Is Smarter Than You Are

You may think that this book you're writing was your idea; it's probably more accurate to suggest that you were the book's idea. After all, it was your book that summoned you to convert its formless energy into form… into words on a page. So discard all notions that you're in charge and give up all pretense at control. You're not the boss. Your book is.

Rule #8
Your Book Is Boss

How did your book get to be boss? Because it's smarter than you are. Because it knows what it's about better than you ever will. Because it's the book's story you are writing, not yours. Given that, you might as well forget everything you think you know about the book, including all preconceptions about its form, structure and content.

Instead, approach your book with an open heart and an open mind. Don't force your will onto it. Talk to it. Sit in the silence with it. Listen to it. Follow its lead. Let it have its way with you. If you do, it will write itself for you.

Explorations

Ask yourself these questions and don't think about the answers. Let them emerge freely and honestly…on the Muse Stream, where appropriate:
- Where have I been assuming that I know best? Where have I been resisting my book's superior wisdom?
- Where have I been openly defying my book and Muse?
- What preconceptions about my book have I been clinging to? How can I begin to let them go?
- Where have I been pushing my book rather than letting myself be pulled by it?
- Where in my relationship with my book can I be more openhearted and surrendered?
- In what other ways can I let my book be boss?

Try This Too

Revisit the centering meditation from Rule #2, but this time feel yourself releasing more and more control of your book *to* your book with each breath.

Tales of the Unexpected

As you grow to surrender to the superior wisdom of your book, you may find that you have been tricked into writing and discovering the unexpected, the undesired, the unwanted. That's because of Rule #9.

Rule #9

Your Book Is a Trickster

The Trickster is a mythological and archetypal figure that dupes its victims into doing its bidding. Mischievous by nature, it will lie unashamedly and break any rule to get its own way.

In myth, think leprechauns (Ireland), coyotes (U.S. Southwest), the Greek god Dionysus and the Hawaiian/Polynesian demigod Maui. In literature and popular culture, think *A Midsummer Night's Dream*'s Puck, *King Lear*'s Fool (along with every court jester ever conceived), Q in *Star Trek: The Next Generation*, Bart Simpson, the Pink Panther and Bugs Bunny.

Your book and Muse are also tricksters. As you craft the book you think you are writing, they will often trick you into writing something you never expected to write, something you never thought you wanted to write, something, perhaps, that is uncomfortable to write.

This is good.

Curse, mutter and resist if you must. Then give in. Your book *is* smarter than you are and it will always take you not only to the place of creative magic, awe and wonder but to the place where your book's ideal expression resides…if you get out of the way and let it.

Let it.

Explorations

Ask yourself these questions and don't think about the answers. Let them emerge freely and honestly…on the Muse Stream, where appropriate:
- Where has my book surprised me? Shocked me? Scared me?
- Where has my book tricked me?
- Where has my book propelled me out of my comfort zone? Did I resist? How?

- In what other unexpected directions has my book pushed me? Was I able to surrender gracefully or did I resist? If I resisted, in what ways can I commit to surrendering more quickly and gracefully next time?
- What unexpected and/or disturbing things am I discovering through this book-birthing experience? About the book? About myself?

Relax: It's Only Your First (or Second or Third) Draft

"When people see the nice books with the nice white pages and the nice black writing," Margaret Atwood has said, "what they don't see is the chaos and the complete frenzy and general shambles that the work comes out of."

Writing is an act of creating something out of nothing. It's the process of converting primordial sludge into art. It's the Godlike feat of shaping words and worlds out of a formless void. And if Genesis makes throwing together a finished world in six days look easy, it's probably because it edited out the frenzied bits that Atwood talks about.

Creation is messy work. From first draft to last, it's anything but orderly.

Rule #10

Embrace the Chaos

In fiction, characters change their names, ages and genders at will, transforming themselves from protagonists to antagonists or from bit players to leads for reasons known only to them. Plots pretzel around and in on themselves multiple times over, leading you, the writer, on a bewildering journey that only begins to make sense once it has ended.

In nonfiction, premises, themes and conclusions pull you into a demented square dance, switching partners and direction on you with mind-twisting frequency.

In both, first chapters become final chapters, final chapters get edited out, restored and edited out again, and middle bits get rewritten until they are unrecognizable, only to become books of their own.

It wasn't until I was halfway through my first draft of *The SunQuest*, for example, that I discovered why I had felt the need to excise large chunks of *The StarQuest* after its first draft. I had written those scenes for the wrong story. They turned out to be part of *The SunQuest*. (Moral: Keep your outtakes.)

Trust the disorderly process that is at the root of all creative acts. Free your characters. Free your plots. Free your narrative. Embrace the chaos. Let your book's natural order emerge organically, not through any act of will on your part. Which will bring us to Rule #11, as soon as you answer a few questions.

EXPLORATIONS

Ask yourself these questions and don't think about the answers. Let them emerge freely and honestly…on the Muse Stream, where appropriate:
- In general, how do I experience chaos in my creative pursuits? How well do I handle it?
- What has been chaotic about my experiences with this book I'm birthing? Do I handle it gracefully or with stress and anxiety?
- How can I flow more easily with Margaret Atwood's "complete frenzy and general shambles" and embrace the chaos inherent in all creative acts?

Your Book is Out of Order

Like movies, which are rarely filmed in sequence, your first (or second or third) draft may not write itself in final book order. *Birthing Your Book* certainly didn't.

In this as in all aspects of your book-writing enterprise, let the bits and pieces of your book come as they come…and write them that way, knowing that the book's innate wisdom will determine the appropriate order when the time is right.

Rule #11
It's All in Order…Even If It's Not

Sometimes, writing a chapter, scene or segment out of sequence — intentionally or not — can reveal to you aspects of your book's theme, premise or, in fiction, characters that you might otherwise have overlooked or have taken longer to discover.

Sometimes, too, postponing a challenging part of your book can help keep you writing when you hit a roadblock.

Follow the Muse Stream where it takes you and don't second-guess your book-directed creative journey.

Kicking the Perfectionism Habit

Whether in writing or in life, many of us are addicted to perfectionism. Being perfect, we believe, guarantees that we will never be criticized, judged, rejected, shamed or humiliated. Being perfect means getting it right in a single draft. Being perfect means a cutthroat auction for our completed manuscript, resulting in a six-figure/six-book deal with a major publisher, instant *New York Times*-bestseller status and an endorsement by Oprah.

Okay, so that single-draft opus and six-figure deal may not happen (right away) and Oprah might not notice you until your second book. But being perfect is, well, still a good thing to be. Isn't it?

It might be if it were possible. It isn't. No matter how hard you try and how many drafts you churn out, your book will never be perfect. Never. Not ever.

Rule #12

Your Book Is Perfect…Even If It's Not

Your book may be excellent, accomplished, creative and insightful. It may be brilliant, compelling and universally lauded. But perfect? Not possible.

It's not possible because when we translate an idea or concept into language, we're taking something that is infinite (energy) and dynamic (neural impulses) and converting it into something that is finite (language) and static (squiggles on a page). The resulting "translation" can never be more than an approximation.

Can you describe the most stunning sunset you have ever experienced in words that accurately and precisely convey to me every shade and nuance of what you saw and felt? Of course you can't. Until we can link a USB cable from your writer-brain to my reader-brain, that translation will remain imprecise and imperfect — more an Impressionist painting than a hyperreal photograph.

That's okay. Those spaces between your Impressionist brushstrokes free me as reader to have my own experience of your sunset, an experience that will be as personal to me as other readers' will be to them.

Perfection is not possible in any creative endeavor. It's not possible in any human endeavor. It's just not possible. As Salvador Dali once said, "Have no fear of perfection, you'll never reach it."

Don't beat yourself up — or your book — because it isn't perfect. Accept the inherent imperfection that is the perfection of all creative enterprise and when you have done the best you can, let this book go and move on to your next one.

Explorations

Ask yourself these questions and don't think about the answers. Let them emerge freely and honestly…on the Muse Stream, where appropriate:

- Am I surrendering to the Muse Stream as I write, or am I going back over sentences and paragraphs trying to perfect them? *If it's the former, keep up the good work and find a way to celebrate the achievement. If it's the latter, revisit Rule #4.*
- Am I judging what I write to be not good enough? *If so, notice your judgments, don't judge yourself for them and do your best to keep writing — through and past your judgment. If you need help getting to a place of non-judgment, jump ahead to the "Let Judgment Go" meditation in Section 5.*

The Voice of Discernment

Judgment is a blunt hammer, a judge's gavel. It knocks you out with a "Guilty" or spares you with an "Innocent."

You need subtler skills and more refined tools as you conceive, create and release your book. You need Rule #13. You need discernment.

Rule #13
Practice Discernment

Discernment is a delicate tool, a marriage of intuition and intellect, a blend of right and left brain, a meld of heart and mind, a whole-body approach to writing and to life.

There is no good or bad and no right or wrong in discernment. There are no harsh comparisons. There is inner knowingness, a heart-centered weighing of merits, a gentle, loving, compassionate approach.

There is no crusade for perfection in discernment, simply the moment-to-moment quest for excellence.

There are no extremes of black and white in discernment. There are no absolute certainties. There is simply the voice of your heart, the voice your Muse, the voice of your book.

Practice listening to that voice. Practice trusting that voice. Practice living and writing in the zone of no-absolutes, that infinite zone between the certainties of black and white, which is the only zone where creation, innovation and life can thrive and grow.

Is Your Write Book the Right Book?

A good idea for a book isn't always the right idea for *your* book. Don't write the book you think you should write. Write the book you know can't not write. Write the book no one else can write.

RULE #14

Write *Your* Right Book

There are many great ideas for books out there. Your friends will suggest them. Your neighbors will suggest them. Your kids and colleagues will suggest them. Anyone who knows you're a writer will suggest them.

The most tempting suggestions, however, will come from your logical mind. Here's how it works: You see something online, in a newspaper or magazine or on TV or you overhear something in a store or cafe, and your logical mind insists that it has the makings of the Oprah-lauded, *New York Times* bestseller we talked about in Rule #12.

Maybe it does. Maybe it doesn't.

Maybe it's yours to write. Maybe it isn't.

There's a difference between a good idea and the right idea, between an idea that is anyone's for the taking and one that is uniquely yours.

Before you launch into a frenzy of book-birthing, ask yourself these questions:

- Is this the book I feel called to write, the book I'm passionate about, the book only I can write? Or is this anyone's book?
- Is this another good idea or is this the right write idea for me?

Anyone can take a good idea and give it shape and substance. Some can do it better than you, some not as well.

No one can take the idea that has impassioned you and perform the kind of alchemy on it that you can. Only you can transform that idea into the one-of-a-kind gem it longs to be. That is why this book, through your Muse, called to you…chose you.

Accept that you were chosen. Perform your magic. Let your right book be the book you write.

Right now.

EXPLORATIONS

Ask yourself these questions and don't think about the answers. Let them emerge freely and honestly…on the Muse Stream, where appropriate:
- How easy is it for me to respond honestly to others' suggestions and expectations?
- Do I have people-pleasing tendencies that have found their way into what and how I write? Into how I relate to others about my work?
- How well can I discern the difference between a good idea and the right idea?
- How easy is it for me to trust my discernment?
- Is the book I'm writing or contemplating writing the right write idea for me?

It's Not Always Time to Write

Sometimes, even the right idea is not the write idea for right now. If you have written as deeply into your book as you can and you find yourself unable to continue, don't label yourself blocked. Perhaps you need more life experience, more research or a stretch of time with a different writing project before you are ready to move forward with this one.

Use your discernment to know whether you are blocked or unnecessarily distracted, or whether its time to walk away — for a time or for all time.

If it's for a time, welcome the break…to research, to work on something else or to get on with your life, trusting that you will know when it's time to return to your book. If it's for all time, recognize that no words you write are ever wasted. They are simply stepping stones on the journey to better words, a better draft or a better book.

RULE #15
Write What's Right for You Right Now

I was about a hundred manuscript pages into my first draft of *The MoonQuest* when my life turned itself — and me — upside-down. As I write in *Acts of Surrender: A Writer's Memoir*, I found myself, at age 39, selling off most everything I owned and leaving Toronto with my few remaining possessions crammed into my car. Destination: three Canadian provinces and a thousand miles away in Nova Scotia, where I knew no one and was set to birth a new life. Packed away in the bowels of my car were my *MoonQuest* notes and pages.

It would be five months before I dug out the box and retrieved the manuscript.

A damp, wintry wind was gusting off the white-capped waters of Pubnico Harbour the afternoon I placed my stack of *MoonQuest* pages on a corner of my kitchen table. I stared at the manuscript through dinner that night, breakfast the next morning and lunch the following noon, not daring to touch it. Thing is, I was terrified to read those hundred pages. I was afraid the manuscript wasn't any good. I was also afraid that, through my months of transformative upheaval, I had outgrown the book and would have no choice but to abandon it.

With lunch that second day over, I gingerly picked up the printed pages and carried them to my favorite armchair. Optimist that I was, I also brought a pen and notepad with me.

What I realized, once I let myself begin reading, was that, even without Nova Scotia, I could never have continued with *The MoonQuest* all those months earlier. I hadn't been ready. The story had been more mature than I was — emotionally, spiritually and creatively. That's why the book had cut me off when it did.

As it turned out, those five world-altering months gave me the life experience I needed in order to catch up with the story and carry on. I began writing the moment I finished reading, and three months and three hundred additional pages later, I dropped the final period on that first draft.

If your discernment guides you to let your book go, don't mourn the perceived waste of time and energy. Trust that you will either return to it when the time is right or that you have gained all you needed from the experience and can now move on to other writing.

A right idea is not necessarily right for all time, nor is a wrong one always wrong for all time. But if it's wrong for right now, let it go and free yourself to write what's right. For you. Now.

Try This

Writing on the Muse Stream in your *Birthing Your Book* journal, explore your answers to these questions:
- Am I writing the book that is right for me right now?
- Am I forcing a book to completion when, perhaps, it's time to let it go for now…or for good?
- How can I be more discerning…about my book, about my passion, about my timing?

What Do Publishers Want?

Unless you have insider access to a breaking news story and can whip off a polished manuscript in a few days, ignore today's market trends.

Rule #16
Market Trends Are Irrelevant

The manuscripts that agents and publishers seek today are unlikely to be the same ones they will be snapping up by the time you have finished your book. The market is volatile. Agents are fickle. Publishers are capricious. Today's trends rarely resemble tomorrow's.

On the other hand, the book your heart calls to you to write in this moment may be just what captures an agent's attention in a year or two. The book your Muse sends you today may be just the one that makes a publisher's pulse race when it crosses his or her desk some time after that.

Write the book you must write right now, and trust the book and your Muse to find its right home in its right time.

Write. Right?

Many books and teachers insist that you know what you're writing about before you start. I say, you don't have to know your book's theme or thrust in order to begin. All you have to do is begin, surrendering to one word after the next until you're finished. All you have to do is write.

RULE #17
Write!

If this seems the most obvious of my rules, it isn't. It's easy to put writing aside in favor of research. It's even easier to put writing aside while you try to figure out what this book that is calling to you is all about.

There is nothing to figure out. There is only this word and then this one and then this one.

Don't wait to figure out what your book is about. Don't worry about its direction, theme, structure or focus. Don't worry about chapter breaks (my first *MoonQuest* draft had none). Don't worry about what people will think of it, or of you. Don't worry about anything. Set pen to paper or fingers to keyboard and, without judging or second-guessing what emerges, let your book do its wizardly work — on you as much as on the page.

Write what comes as it comes. Whatever it is. If you let its sentences flow freely through you and surrender to it unconditionally, you will learn all you need to know about your book through the writing of it.

Should your book's direction change along the way — or should its theme, structure or focus change — don't fight it. Surrender to the moment. Surrender to the book you are writing in each moment. Your book knows what it's doing.

In other words: Write…the book you didn't know you had in you…the book you could never have imagined writing…the book you believed you could not write…the book that is yours to write.

TRY THIS

You know what to do. Don't wait for the perfect moment that will never come. Don't wait until you have one, two or five free hours. Don't wait for the perfect book idea or the perfect opening sentence. Don't wait until you have an outline. Don't wait until you take a writing class. Don't wait until you finish reading *Birthing Your Book*. Don't wait for your kids to grow up. Don't wait for your retirement. *Now* is the best time to write. So write!

Are Your Goals Working for You?

Whenever I take on new coaching or mentoring clients, I always end the first session by asking, "How much time can you realistically devote to your book over the next week?" Whatever the answer, I inevitably insist that they cut it in half.

It's human nature to set overambitious goals. It's also what we're taught in school and what we're encouraged to do by most writing coaches, books, seminars and workshops.

Unfortunately, it's also human nature to judge ourselves harshly when we don't achieve those goals.

At best, when we miss our target, we hold to the original goal and try again. At worst, we lower our expectations. In neither case do we feel good about what we have accomplished. In both cases, we mourn our inadequacy rather than celebrating whatever it was we managed to write.

Isn't it better to set a one-page-per-week goal and get it done rather than to aim for thirty and end up only having written one?

You may ask: "If the creative output is the same under both scenarios, what difference does it make?" The difference is how we feel about what we have accomplished…or not accomplished.

In the first situation, we feel sensational — about ourselves and about our book-in-progress. We feel as though we have succeeded.

In the second, we feel discouraged, and our perceived failure could continue to haunt and disable us as we move ahead with the book.

Rule #18
Set Yourself Up for Success

Set yourself up for success not for failure by giving yourself ridiculously easy goals and meeting them, easily. If that means committing to fifty words per writing session, that's fine. Set your goal and meet it. Then build on that success by gradually increasing your goal.

It's important to build up a sense of the possible, to continue proving to yourself that your book is doable. Applying unrealistic goals that you fail to meet only underlines your difficulties with your book and fuels discouragement. Instead, let each success breed more confidence and each confidence, more success.

Set yourself up for success, and before you know it, you will be dropping the ultimate period on the final draft of your book.

Oh, and don't forget to celebrate each success. Too often, we ignore our successes and focus only on what we have failed to achieve.

Try This

Have you set yourself an overambitious writing goal that you are challenged to meet? It could be a word-count goal or it could be a time goal. Whichever it is, cut it by half or more — enough that you can achieve it easily.

As you meet your new goal, find a meaningful way to honor yourself for your success. Then increase the goal bit by bit, either from one day to the next or one week to the next.

Try This Too

Too often, when we reach the end of our writing day, we lament all that we have failed to accomplish. Rarely, do we celebrate what we have achieved.

Tonight, as you inventory your day, ignore any goal unreached and all tasks left undone. Instead, run through your day and acknowledge everything you achieved, however seemingly inconsequential. Don't limit this exercise to your book project. Include *everything*.

Continue this inventory in your *Birthing Your Book* journal for at least two weeks. As the days progress, notice how your focus evolves from your perceived failures and not-good-enoughs toward your real successes and attainments.

At the end of each week, pick your most outstanding accomplishment and celebrate it.

Acts of Commitment

What does commitment mean? It means making your book a priority in your life. It means not letting fear, excuses or distractions divert you from listening for the voice of your Muse and surrendering to the call of your book. It means letting the ideas of your heart find expression through your mind. It means trusting that your book knows the way and trusting it to guide you from first page to last. It means honoring your passion and respecting yourself.

RULE #19

Commit to Yourself as the Writer You Are

What about discipline? I'm glad you asked. You'll find your answer in Section 5, in "The Heart of Discipline."

EXPLORATIONS

Ask yourself these questions and don't think about the answers. Let them emerge freely and honestly…on the Muse Stream, where appropriate:
- In what ways do I fail to treat my book as a priority in my life?
- How else am I not honoring my passion to write?
- What steps can I take, today, to strengthen my commitment to my book, to my creativity, to my passion? To myself?

Rules? What Rules?

It's been a long time since Rule #1, so…

RULE #20

There Are No Rules

This is the one rule that never changes. No matter what you're writing, the only certainties are that flow is fluid, your creation is unique and your book makes its own rules. Truly, there is no universal right way or wrong way. There is only your way, the way of your book.

TRY THIS

Pull together some art supplies, call in your inner artist and create a large banner for your writing area that reads *Rule #1: There Are No Rules!* When your masterpiece is complete, post it somewhere that is always visible when you write. Also consider scanning it to use as your computer screen's wallpaper.

5. Creation

*Every stroke of my brush
is the overflow
of my inmost heart.*
Sengai, Buddhist monk

I have no control over my writing. I have lots of good intentions, but no control. There's a story that wants to be told.
Urusla K. Le Guin, novelist

Genesis

"God said, 'Let there be light,' and there was light."

Your act of creation is like God's in Genesis, an act of allowance, of letting…of surrender.

Surrender to the book that has chosen you to write it. Surrender to how it chooses to be written. Surrender to the light of its superior wisdom.

Just as the Creator in most religious and spiritual traditions allows you the free will to live your imperative and forge your story through the living of it, your highest call is to allow the book that now leaps from your heart, mind and vision that same freedom.

Your job as author-creator is to *let* the energy of your book emerge into form from formlessness and to breathe life into it that it may experience all it has come onto your page to live…that you may experience all that you have joined up with it to live.

Let there be light…and there will be.

Let your book take form, and it will.

Your Book Chose You

You believe that you came up with the idea for this book. You believe that you chose this book to write. You could not be more wrong.

Your book chose you.

Your book, which has existed as a strand of energy since the time before time, determined that no one but you could to take the incorporeal weave of infinity that it has always been and make it tangible and finite.

Your book chose you to take it from its purest state — abstract, discarnate and ethereal — and convert it into the squiggles on a page we call language…something physical, something you and I can touch, something you and I can hold. Something you and I can read.

Your book chose you because it needs you. It needs you to give it a life it could not otherwise have.

You also need your book — to give you a life you could not otherwise have.

You need it because just as you are birthing this book, this book is birthing you.

Whoever you were when you first surrendered to its call is not who you will be when the book is complete. Just as its form will have altered, so will yours have. Not physically, perhaps, but in every other way of significance. You cannot write from a place of heart and have it any other way.

Writing is an act of transformation. Each word you free onto the page carries the potential to change you in ways you cannot now imagine. This is even truer for the words you did not expect to write…for the book you did not expect to write, the book you did not expect to birth through you.

The more you surrender to those changes, the more easily your book will write itself for you. The more you resist them, the more you will find yourself resisting the words that would otherwise leap easily from heart to hand to page.

Surrender to the journey, your journey, and let your book perform its alchemy on you. Surrender to the journey and experience the magic — on the page and in your life — that only acts of creation can ignite.

Writing Through the Fog

Just because you think you know what your book is about when you begin doesn't mean that you're right.

"I didn't know what my memoir was about until I finished my first draft," author Karen Walker has confessed about her award-nominated *Following the Whispers*. I had a similar experience with *Acts of Surrender: A Writer's Memoir*.

So often, the book we are writing is wiser than we are. So often, our creativity begins the moment we abandon control and, instead, let its story direct us.

Novelist E.L. Doctorow writes, "Writing is like driving at night in the fog. You can only see as far as your headlights, but you can make the whole trip that way."

As we move forward, writing the word or sentence we know, the next will always appear…if we are open to it. If we have our eyes on the road and our headlights on, if we are prepared to trust in the unknown that lies just beyond the reach of our vision, that unknown will become illuminated, known and manifest.

There's a scene in my novel *The MoonQuest* that reminds me of Doctorow's quote. In it, the main character is walking a celestial road that only forms as he steps forward. The road behind him is gone and the road beyond each next step cannot be discerned. As stressful and discomfiting as he finds the journey, the road takes him where he needs to go, to a place he could never have imagined.

Ironically, that's the same journey I traveled in writing *The MoonQuest*, a book whose story I knew nothing about except as I wrote it. Some days Doctorow's headlights showed me the next scene. Some days, they showed me only the next sentence. Some days, only the next word. Yet as I surrendered to the journey and to the voice of the book, the story unfolded, magnificently, and in ways I could never have predicted, plotted, outlined or envisioned.

At the same time, be aware that your trickster of a book will do whatever it takes to get the ultimate story out of you, the story *it* wants you to tell, even if there's deception involved. Remember Book-Birthing Rule #9? Karen Walker began her book thinking she was writing one story. The memoir that emerged was something else altogether. It was also more insightful and compelling than anything she could have consciously dreamed up.

Let go all preconceptions, assumptions and expectations about what your book is or should be, and trust that it will reveal its true nature to you in the writing of it. Let your book have its own life through you, and trust that its innate wisdom will weave the narrative that will best serve it, serve you and serve your readers. Surrender to that innate wisdom. Get out of your book's way (get out of *your* way) and let the story tell itself through you.

As Stephen King points out in *On Writing: A Memoir of the Craft*, "I am, after all, not just the novel's creator but its first reader. And if I'm not able to guess with any accuracy how the damned thing is going to turn out, even with my inside knowledge of coming events, I can be pretty sure of keeping the reader in a state of page-turning anxiety. And why worry about the ending anyway? Why be such a control freak? Sooner or later every story comes out somewhere."

Explorations

Ask yourself these questions and don't think about the answers. Let them emerge freely and honestly…on the Muse Stream, where appropriate:

- How much control do I cling to in this book I am writing?
- Where I can let go some of that control and trust that the story — the one I'm living as much as the one I'm writing — knows best?
- Where in my creative and life's journey can I more fully trust that the headlights illuminating my way will carry me to my unseen and unimagined destination?
- How can I surrender more fully and graciously to my book's wisdom and imperative?
- What steps can I take in my next writing session to be less controlling and more surrendered?

Write What You Know?

What does it mean to "write what you know"? Does it mean that you can only write your book from direct, personal experience? Or is there a deeper meaning to that clichéd commandment?

I say your book can be about anything, regardless of what you think you know. I say you can write about anybody, regardless of who you are. You can write about men if you're a woman and women if you're a man. You can write about gays and lesbians if you're straight in the same way that gays and lesbians have been writing about heterosexuals for generations. You can write about a lawyer if you're an athlete or about an athlete if you're an astronaut.

You can perform all these literary feats by writing what you know — not what you know from the outside in, which is what that dictum usually suggests, but what you know from the inside out.

You can because we are all one in our humanity and we all draw from the same pool of human emotion — whoever we are and whatever our background. Whoever we are and whatever our background, it's our humanity and emotional life that connect us to our readers, not the dry superficialities of our outward experience.

So you have never experienced the discrimination a black woman or gay man might have felt? Have you ever been attacked for who you are? Have you ever been denied what you believed was rightfully yours? Have you ever felt that your personhood was under attack?

No? Think back to childhood, to the bullies in the schoolyard, to the adults who criticized you. Do more than think back. Relive and re-experience those moments. You *have* lived some of those same emotions you feel you dare not describe in someone else.

So you have never run a marathon or fought a courtroom battle. Have you ever competed for something? For a school prize or award? For a boyfriend or girlfriend? For a job? On the job? Have you experienced the exhilaration of a hard-won success or the heartbreak or humiliation of failure? If you have, you have lived some of what an athlete or lawyer has lived.

Of course, depending on your theme, genre and topic, you may need to conduct some research in order to fill in your experience gaps. But it's not your encyclopedic knowledge that will keep your readers turning the pages of your book. It's your humanity and, where appropriate, your vulnerability. That's what you know, and that is what will touch your readers, that will affect them, that will move them to deeper places within themselves.

It will also, as I have pointed out elsewhere in this book, transform you. You will not only be writing what you know. You will be discovering what you know through your writing.

When we dare to tap into deep, inner places of emotional truth in our writing, what comes out can startle us. More often than is comfortable, it can also force us to reexamine who we are, what we believe, how we live and our place in the world, and to do it through a more sharply focused lens than we have ever before dared employ.

"Most writers write to say something about other people — and it doesn't last," Gloria Steinem writes in *Revolution from Within*. "Good writers write to find out about themselves, and it lasts forever."

Write what you know, then let that journey carry you to all the places within that you didn't know you knew. Write to *discover* what you know, to discover what you believe, to uncover hidden depths within yourself that only emerge when you take a leap of faith onto the blank page and write freely from your heart.

Explorations

Ask yourself these questions and don't think about the answers. Let them emerge freely and honestly…on the Muse Stream, where appropriate:

- Where can I plumb the emotions and experiences that I share with all humanity to write about things I wouldn't before have dared to write about?
- Where can I plumb those same emotions and experiences to go deeper in my book? In all my writing?
- What am I holding myself back from writing because I believe that I don't know enough? Can I let myself open up to discover what I *do* know?
- Where in my book and in all my writing can I write what I know — from the inside out as well as from the outside in?
- Where am I hiding behind the words of my book…from myself and from others?
- Where am I letting myself shine through the words of my book…for myself and for others?
- What am I discovering about myself as I write my book?
- What else would my book reveal to me about *me*, if I let it?

Trust Your Book

Your book is a sentient entity with a life force and wisdom of its own, with a will and imperative of its own. If you trust it to exercise that will and imperative through you, your book-birthing experience will astonish you with its ease and free-flow. If you trust it to guide you through the journey of setting that wisdom onto the page, the book you have felt called to write will appear as if by magic.

Some authors fear that unless they retain an uncompromising grip on their book-birthing experience, the result will be disjointed, inconsistent, thematically uneven and structurally unsound.

I say (again and again): The more you abandon that all-too-human determination to control processes and predict outcomes and, instead, trust your book, the richer and more engaging will be your final manuscript.

A few years ago an artist came to me with the painter's equivalent of writer's block. She sensed a new style birthing through her but didn't know how to access it. All she could do was stare at her blank canvas in mounting frustration.

"Your only job is to hold the brush," I counseled her, "because that's the one thing your painting can never do on its own. If you get out of the way and trust the brush to move your hand across the canvas, your painting will reveal itself to you."

She did, and it did.

It's no different with your book.

In the end, the Muse Stream is about trust. It's about trusting that if you move from the driver's seat of your writing experience to its passenger seat, you will free onto the page a book that is more imaginative, engaging and original than anything you could have consciously thought up.

Creativity — and every book-writing experience is a creative process, regardless of genre, topic or type — is not a logical enterprise you can expect to control.

Creativity is about weird leaps of faith that often make no sense in the moment. In fact, what seems to be nonsense in the moment may turn out to be the most brilliant aspect of your book by the time you type the final period on the final page.

So get out of the way and let your book have its way with you. Get out of the way and let the words spill out of you, the words your book needs, not the words you think it needs. Not the words you think you need.

Abandon control and free your book to live its full potential through you, a potential your conscious imagination can only begin to touch.

Talk to Your Book: A Meditative Journey

If your book is a sentient entity, and I continue to insist that it is, why not ask it what it needs from you? Wouldn't that be more effective than trying to figure out what it's about on your own? Using the same meditative dialogue technique I refer to in "Revelations" (Section 3), the same one that produced "Dialogues with the Divine: Encounters with Your Wisest Self," you can enter into a conversation with the essence and spirit of your book and get all the guidance and information you need.

ALLOW AT LEAST 30 MINUTES FOR THIS MEDITATIVE EXERCISE
AND FOR THE WRITING EXPERIENCE THAT FLOWS FROM IT.

Have pen and paper, tablet or laptop handy, or sit as comfortably as you can at your desk or computer table.

Settle into a physical, emotional and spiritual state of stillness. If you have a meditation practice, do whatever you normally do to get into a receptive space. If not, close your eyes and sit quietly, focusing on your breath to quiet your mind.

Use music, aromatherapy, crystals, yoga or ritual if you find any or all of these to be helpful. You can also use the "Inside Your Book" meditation in the next chapter to both relax you and help guide you through the experience.

If you are unable to still your mind, don't worry about it. Writing your mind-chatter will give it voice and, ultimately, silence it.

Write the first thought about your book that comes to mind. It can be a question or feeling. It can be a statement of praise or complaint. It can be the voice of your inner critic, your fear or your inner child. It can be nattering mind noise. Whatever it is, write your side of the conversation, then let a response emerge spontaneously onto the page. Don't look for an answer. Don't think about an answer. *Let* the answer.

The key, in both sides of your conversation, is to write on the Muse Stream — without stopping, without thinking, without correcting spelling, punctuation or grammar and, most particularly, without censoring or second-guessing. In doing so, you will write through and past any judgment or fear and you will discover what you already knew about your book but didn't know you knew.

Continue your dialogue for as long as you feel the need to and then a little longer after that. The wisest words and deepest truths often emerge after we think we're finished.

If you get stuck, revisit "Help, I'm Stuck" in Section 2.

- *Adapt this exercise to "interview" your characters if you're writing fiction. You can use it, too, to deepen your awareness of scenes and settings, for they, too, have a kind of sentience.*

Inside Your Book: A Guided Meditation

<small>Allow at least 40 minutes for this meditation
and for the writing experience that flows from it.</small>

Get comfortable and close your eyes. Take a deep breath in, and let it go. Take another. Let that go. As you breathe in and out, let your shoulders drop and feel the muscles in your arms and neck relax. Feel your whole body relax.

With each inhalation, breathe in more deeply and feel yourself breathing in to the essence of this book you are writing or are getting ready to write, to the essence of your creativity, to the essence of your creative power, to the powerful essence of you.

With each exhalation, feel more and more of the tension dissolve from your body. Feel all the anxiety dissolve from your body. Feel all the emotional strain and stress dissolve from your body. Let your shoulders drop some more, and feel nothing but peace and calm envelope you.

Be in the moment with that peace. Be in the moment with your breath. Be one with your breath, so that the only thing you are aware of in this instant *is* this instant…is the essence of this instant and, within that essence of the moment, the essence of your book, a book that has called to you so strongly for so long…a book whose call you have now, finally, answered.

What is this book? It is the book that you are now writing or will soon be writing. It is the finished book that already exists whole and complete in its own infinite and invisible realm. It is the completed book that is waiting for you to engage with it, that is waiting for you to trust it. That is waiting for you to surrender to it.

So, acknowledge that your book knows itself better than you do, that your book knows itself better than you ever will. Acknowledge that and open your heart and mind to all that the story of your book and the book of your story have to offer you now through this experience.

Continue to focus on your breath. Continue to go deep within. As you do, as you let your breath carry you deep into your heart and deep into the heart of your book, allow an image, any image, to bubble up into your conscious awareness, an image that represents the energy of your book, the energy of your story.

This image need not make conventional sense. There's a good chance that it won't. It could be a color. It could be a person. It could be an animal. It could be a sound. It be an object; it could even be or look like a book...but don't force it to look like a book. Or it could simply be a feeling.

Whatever it is, whatever it looks like, let it bubble up into your awareness. Don't judge it. Don't censor it. Let it emerge and, whatever it is, be okay with it.

Be aware, too, that if this is a repeat meditative experience with the same book and story, a different image may emerge for you now than emerged last time. That's okay. Go with whatever bubbles up for you today.

We are dealing with a nonphysical energy and with your mind's representation of that energy. We are also dealing with your evolving relationship with your book. It's natural for your imagery to evolve as well.

Trust today's representation of that energy. Trust tomorrow's, too, if it shows up differently. Trust that whatever emerges whenever it emerges is perfect for who you are in the moment you intuit and discern it, is perfect for your relationship with your book right now.

Before you begin to converse or connect with that image, if you haven't already, begin to get a sensory sense of it. Begin to use your senses to help you connect more fully and deeply with that essence, with that energy — with the essence and energy your book — through the image that has emerged for you today.

Get a sense of color, if there's color.

Get a sense of shape, if there's shape.

Get a sense of depth, if there's depth.

Get a sense of texture, if there's texture.

Which other of your senses is awakened by it? Smell? Taste? Sound? Music, perhaps?

What about your nonphysical senses? Your emotional senses?

If the image in any way resembles a book, note its size, shape and thickness, the colors and textures of its cover. Note any images on the cover. Note any text — a title? your name as author? — and note the size, color and font of the text.

Whatever this physical representation of the spirit and essence of your book is, not all your physical and emotional senses may apply to it, but they may. Or those that are not relevant today may be relevant on a different day, or in a different, perhaps unconventional way.

What does this image look like to you right now, even as you know that it could change in the next moment? What does it feel like? If it feels powerful, don't let yourself feel overwhelmed by that power. Know that that power is you, and that that power is an expression not only of the book's essence but of your essence. Not only of the book's story, but of your story.

Whatever this image is, however you perceive it, whatever its qualities and characteristics, embrace it. Take it in. Breathe it in. Fully. And let your sensory and emotional experience of this image connect you more intimately than ever before with the energy and essence of the story that it represents.

It's time now to listen, to listen to that image, whatever it is. It's time to listen from a deep place deep within you, to listen with your heart to what your book, through this image, has to tell you. You might not hear a conscious message, but something will move through you, however unconsciously. Trust that. And trust that however you experience it is the right and perfect way for you right now.

So, take a few moments now to listen…

Now that you have heard, felt or sensed whatever you have heard, felt or sensed, it's time to ask a question of your book through the intermediary of this image. So silently ask a question. Then silently listen for an answer.

You may hear your answer. You may sense your answer. You may get nothing clear or obvious. Even if your question seems unanswered in this moment, an answer will come in another moment, likely in an unexpected way in an unexpected moment. Trust that.

Ask another question, and wait for another answer.

And another.

If the image representing the energy of your book resembles a book and you are able to do so, open it. Riffle through its pages. What is the paper like? How does it smell? How does it feel? What is its weight?

Is there text on the pages? Are you able to read anything of it? What does it say? How does what it says make you feel?

If relevant, take a few moments for this experience…

Before we complete this journey with your book, your book has a message for you. Perhaps it's reassurance. Perhaps it's something you never thought to ask. Listen for what your book has to say, and hear or feel it in whatever way you hear or feel it.

Finally, let your book offer you some closing words, whatever those words might be today, to help you move forward on the next step of your creative journey with it. Listen for those.

Remember that you have been chosen to bring this energy into the physical in the form of a book. Whatever that may feel like in some moments, that is one of the greatest gifts of your life. Be with that awareness for a moment or two. And feel what that feels like.

Now, once again, be conscious of your breath. Be conscious, too, that this process will not end when you open your eyes, but that the intuitive sensings and messages will continue in the hours, days and weeks ahead…will continue throughout your pilgrimage with this book. Remain open to them. Remain available to them. Trust them.

Be aware now of your physical body, of the physical space you now occupy, as you let your breath return you to full awareness. And when you feel ready, taking all the time you need, gently open your eyes and be fully present, ready to jot down any notes or thoughts from this meditative journey you have just traveled.

The Coppola Method

As writer-director Francis Ford Coppola works on a screenplay, he never looks back over what he has already written and he never rewrites until he is ready to start his next draft.

"You have a lot of doubts when you read in unfinished fragments," Coppola told *Creative Screenwriting* magazine in 2009. "There's almost a hormone that secretes from writers to hate what they're writing, so you get fooled into reworking and changing it."

Surrendering to the Muse Stream, as I wrote here earlier, means going with first thoughts, committing to the page whatever leaps first into your mind, however wacky it might seem. In fact, the wackier it seems, the more likely it is that your inner censor is interfering with your creative process.

"Wacky" is a judgment. It comes from that fearful, second-thoughts, second-guessing part of you that is trying to protect you from straying into dangerous territory, that is afraid you will be judged harshly for what you are about to write.

The Muse Stream — writing without stopping — is designed to bypass that inner critic and get your most creative thoughts onto the page before those logical, analytical, critical, cynical, doubt-filled or judgmental parts of you can stop them.

"It's counterproductive," notes Coppola, "to start judging it before you've allowed the whole trip to take place."

That's the creative reason for surrendering to the Muse Stream. There is also a practical reason.

What if you start your book and, before moving forward to the second chapter, you spend days and weeks polishing, perfecting and otherwise tweaking your first-draft opening chapter?

Nothing wrong with that, right?

Wrong.

Here's why. What if, when you begin your second draft, you realize that your opening chapter is not as brilliant as you had originally thought? What if, as you reread those weeks of work, you realize that not only is it not brilliant, it's not even salvageable? As you hold down the delete key over the entire chapter, you will be thinking of all the time you could have put to better use had you surrendered to the Muse Stream, had you written without going back to rewrite, had you kept moving forward.

There is a time and place for revision and rewriting; it's not while you are in your Muse Stream's creative flow. And as we shall see in Section 8, revision need not be the slash-and-burn, left-brain assault you might have been taught. It can be as intuitive as your acts of creation — and just as effective.

First Drafts

This is a first draft that you write in this moment. This first draft is an opportunity to release your book onto the page using the language of your heart, which may not yet be the perfectly executed language of your perfectly spelled, punctuated and grammared brain. That's okay. Allow it to be okay.

Later, you will revisit, review and revise this draft — using your heart-mind to bring it into closer alignment with your heart-vision.

Now, though, is the time to write, to let your book speak to you and through you. Do that now and, whatever your critical mind might say, what you write will be good enough. It will be better than good enough. It will be yours.

It's easy to judge. It's easy to criticize. It's easy to say, "This isn't good enough," "This can never be good enough," "I'm not good enough," "My idea isn't original enough" or "This book has been written before."

It's particularly easy with first drafts. It's just as easy with final drafts.

The truth is, you are good enough. You are good enough because everyone is good enough. We all carry the seeds of creation within us. Besides, if a book has chosen you to write it, then it is your book to write, which means that you must be good enough to do it. Can you trust that?

Your writing, too, is good enough. It's good enough for this draft. In the next draft you will make it better. The draft after that will be better still. That's what drafts are for.

What about the originality of your idea and your book? Your book chose you, not the other way around. It chose you because the story that is this book cannot cannot be told by anyone else.

Let's you and I and a dozen of our friends go to our favorite restaurant and order the same meal cooked the same way. When we're finished, let's each describe every component of the meal — how it tasted, its texture, its aroma, its temperature, how it felt in the mouth, how it melded with the other tastes, textures and temperatures. Let's each say what the food reminded us of, what it evoked within us. Let's each describe the restaurant similarly. Then let's each tell a story about the food, the restaurant and our time together. Although we will all have shared a common experience, we will each create of it a unique story.

Or ask your siblings, parents or kids to write their version of a significant family event. Each version will be different from every other and all will be different from yours.

Only you can tell your story. Only you can write your book. Only your story and your book will be infused with the singularity of your spirit, your outlook, your history and your heart. And infused as it will be with all those elements that both distinguish you from others and link you to all humanity, your book will be as no other has been, is or ever could be.

Leave judgment to judges who sit on the bench. Leave analysis to the analysts. Leave criticism to the critics. Your mission today is to write, to allow words to spill from you unhindered by judgment, unhampered by not-good-enoughs, uncrippled by comparisons.

You have judged yourself as wanting long enough. Now is the time to let your judgment go and watch the Muse Stream flow.

Try This

Take a break from this book to write on your book. Do it now. Write anything at all, as long as it relates in some way to the book you have been called to write. Write for 5 minutes or 50 but write, doing your best to leave judgment to the judges. Write. Now.

Try This Too

Is it hard for you to free yourself from the pincer grip of judgment? Do you condemn the words you are writing and the words you have already written? Do you savage yourself as their author? If so, turn the page and let all that judgment go!

Let Judgment Go: A Guided Meditation

ALLOW AT LEAST 30 MINUTES TO COMPLETE THIS MEDITATION
AND FOR THE WRITING THAT FLOWS FROM IT.

Breathe. Breathe in the quiet, white light of your creative essence, your divine essence, your Muse. Breathe in your fire, your flame, your being-ness, your God-self. Breathe in the light of who you are, the truth of who you are, the love of who you are.

Breathe in all the light and aloha you are.

Aloha is not only a word that conjures up the gentle swaying of palm trees and hula dancers. Aloha is a consciousness, a state of being, a state of openheartedness, a state of love in its truest, fullest sense.

Breathe in to that openness within you. Breathe it in fully, deeply, completely.

Breathe out any doubts, any fears that you're not good enough, that someone else or anyone else — your friend whose book has already been published, your neighbor who just got an agent — is a more accomplished creator. Breathe that out, for it is not true.

You are creative. You are innately creative. You are inherently creative. Everyone is. And because you are, you can express that creativity through writing, through placing one word after the next onto the written page of the book you are birthing.

Let go of all feelings that you're not good enough. For you are.

Release all feelings that others are better than you. They are not.

You are equal to all and equal to the joyful task at hand, which is expressing the words and passions of your heart in written form, in book form.

You are equal to it, for you were born to it. Every micro-bit, every nano-bit of your being — physical, emotional and spiritual — has been encoded with that will, desire and aptitude to create...to create this book that has called to you...this book whose call you are answering.

You may lack certain skills. Those skills can be learned and practiced. In this moment, skills don't matter nearly as much as heart, intent and choice. You have the former. We all do. And you can tap into the latter two with ease.

Know that and be that.

It's simple. It's simple yet complex, for you are pushing against what may seem like lifetimes of programming.

What has been programmed can be erased — more quickly than the time it took to program into you.

You *are* good enough. You are better than good enough.

Despite what anyone ever said, despite any way in which you were treated — words and actions your conscious mind may have long ago forgotten or buried — despite any or all of these, you are a writer. You are an author. You are the author of the book you are writing or about to write.

You are the book's author and you are good enough. Your words are good enough. Your creations are good enough. Your books are good enough. Better than good enough. For they are the unique expressions of a unique heart that is, even now, opening to the prospect and possibility of finally being free to speak.

Feel that freedom. Open to that freedom. Embrace that freedom. It needn't frighten you. It needn't silence you or close you down. It is safe. For in that freedom lies all the truth of the universe, just as within you lies all the truth of the universe.

So put pen to paper, let fingers dance upon the keyboard and simply begin.

Begin at the beginning.

Let that first word be the God of the Old Testament, who allowed the world to form. "Let there be light," God said. Not "I order and command light." Not "The light must look a certain way, must be a certain brightness."

Creation is an act of allowing, of letting. *Let* there be light. *Let* there be creation. *Let* there be one story and then another. And let the words that best express that story find their own way onto the pages of your book, without any need by you to intervene or get in the way.

Let.

Let the words be.

Let your book be.

Let yourself be.

There is no judging in the act of letting. There is no call to judge. There is no call to take any active role whatsoever. Surrender to creation and let it be.

The God of Genesis didn't say as the earth formed, "You know, I don't like this island over here and that mountain over there." God allowed the earth to form and saw it, and it was good. God didn't judge it to be good. By allowing, it was good. Inherently good.

Allow your book to form without judgment, and it, too, will be good.

Give your book life. Then give it the free will to form as it will, to live its imperative.

Let.

Let it form.

Let it be.

Let it love you.

Let yourself love it back.

There is no need to judge. There is never any need to judge.

Let the words flow, and let judgment go. Let it fly...far, far away where it can do no more damage or harm to you or your words or your book. Or to anyone or anything.

Now, pick a word, any word.

Let a word or phrase bubble up into your consciousness. A word that expresses your state of beingness in this moment.

Don't judge it. Never judge.

Don't censor it. Never censor.

Allow.

Simply allow.

And when that word or phrase has emerged, let that be your starting point, your launching pad, your rocket propelling you to the farthest reaches of the universe in a free-flowing flight of creation.

And so, write.

Right now.

Remember to keep your pen moving across the page. Remember to *let* it move across the page. Free it and it will free you.

Let it fly and let yourself fly with it.

If you feel stuck, just keep going. Repeat. Free-associate. Write nonsense. Breathe. Doodle. Any or all of these will release the stuckness and propel you forward.

Write for as long as you can, until you feel complete...and then for a little bit longer if that feels right.

Write.

Now.

- *A version of my recording of this meditation is included — along with ten other, equally inspiring tracks — on "The Voice of the Muse Companion: Guided Meditations for Writers." Look for it on Amazon, iTunes and Google Play and from other online music sellers.*

6. Craft

Follow your hunches. Your hunch is creation.
Frank Capra, writer/director

If there is a magic in story writing, and I am convinced that there is, no one has ever been able to reduce it to a recipe that can be passed from one person to another.
John Steinbeck, novelist

Take Your Time

In the Bible, it is said that God created heaven and earth in six days. Fortunately, you are not likely to be working to the same deadline.

Let your book and its worlds take all the time they need to develop, mature and reveal themselves to you.

If my first draft of *The MoonQuest* took me five months over the course of a year to complete, my first draft of *The StarQuest* took eleven years and two false starts. By contrast, my initial draft of *The SunQuest* took only three weeks.

Remember, creation is a process. Don't feel you must know every last detail before you begin. Don't let the little you think you know overwhelm you and prevent you from moving forward.

Begin your story. If it has characters, let them emerge. Let all aspects of your book reveal themselves to you in the writing. Use the concepts and techniques throughout this book to fill any relevant gaps you perceive as you proceed with your first draft and subsequent drafts. Use them as breaks from storytelling. Use them between drafts. Use them as tools for enrichment. Don't obsess or allow yourself to feel inadequate.

Discover what you can, express what you can and let the rest go. Do your best, take your time…and keep writing!

Into the Heart of Discipline

"What about discipline?" you ask. "You've been talking about intuition and discernment, about trusting my book and my Muse. But every other book I read insists that unless I'm disciplined, I'll never finish my book. What do you say to that?"

A lot.

Let's start with the word "discipline." Its primary definition in *The Oxford English Dictionary* goes like this: "the practice of training people to obey rules or a code of behavior, using punishment to correct disobedience." Then there are the word's origins: from the Middle English, meaning "mortification by scourging oneself."

Punishment? Disobedience? Mortification? Scourging? Is that how you choose to experience this book you are writing?

Yes, most writing books and teachers equate productivity and success with discipline. The problem is that they define discipline, *Oxford*-like, as an ironclad routine that churns out a certain number of words or pages per day, generally produced during the same time period each day.

That's not how I view discipline. As I see it, there are two types a writer can adopt: conventional or "hard" discipline, or what I call "heart" discipline.

Hard discipline, as *The Oxford Dictionary* suggests, is punishing and rule-bound, threatening creative catastrophe should you stray from a strict, butt-in-the-chair routine. Hard discipline is disempowering and mistrustful because it suggests that you lack the commitment to write and the discernment to know when to write. Hard discipline makes it easy to feel shamed, less-than, not-good-enough and blocked.

Heart discipline is different. Heart discipline fosters discernment, intuition and practice. Heart discipline nurtures passion and commitment. Heart disciplines knows no fixed rules, times or goals. Heart discipline is fluid and in-the-moment. Heart disciplines places your Muse and your book in charge of your creative enterprise.

Heart discipline says *trust*. Trust that when you sit down to write, whenever you sit down, your Muse will be there for you. Trust that all you hear, including that it is either time to write or time to stop, is true. Trust that all the pages that flow through you on a given day, be they five or fifty, are the right ones for that day.

Heart discipline is about discipleship. It's about you becoming a disciple — to your passion, to your Muse and to your book. It is not about forcing a creative vision that is boundless in nature to hew to the constraints of a controlling mind or to be constricted by a conventional wisdom that is generally more conventional than it is wise.

Like intuition and discernment, trust is a practice. Practice listening to what's inside you — to the voice of your Muse, the voice of your passion, the voice of your vision and the voice of your book — not to the judgmental, fear-based voices clamoring inside your head or to the disciplinary voices preaching at you from everywhere else.

What if you have no passion for the book you're writing? Then you're writing the wrong book.

Write what impassions, electrifies and enlivens you. Write the book you *must* write. Commit to that book with all your heart and you will never lack the discipline to get it onto the page.

Explorations

Ask yourself these questions and don't think about the answers. Let them emerge freely and honestly…on the Muse Stream, where appropriate:

- How do I define discipline? How does that definition feel as I apply it to my writing day?
- How would the time spent with my book feel if my discipline was less hard and more heart?
- How can I foster the trust that would free me from hard discipline and let my passion propel me forward? What can I do today, now, to begin to foster that trust?
- How passionate am I about this book I'm writing? How can I nurture and feed that passion?
- How can I begin to more fully express and experience my commitment — to my book and to myself as the writer I am?

Try This

It's time to revisit Book-Birthing Rule #18: Set Yourself Up for Success. If you have not yet set easily achievable goals for you and your book-writing project, now is the time to do it.

Remember that the point is not to set targets so ambitious that it would take superhuman effort to meet them. The point is to make it easy for you to succeed, to build on your successes by gradually toughening your goals and to celebrate each success!

Whose Book Are You Writing?

A few years ago, I was listening to a guest speaker — let's call him Tom — at a writer's group. He was talking about characters.

"In the first half of your story," he counseled, "let your characters do what they want. But when you get to the second half, you've got to rein them in."

Tom was adamant, and it took all the self-control I possessed to rein myself in…not because of the first half of his statement, but because of the second — and not only as it applies to characters in fictional stories but as it applies to our books themselves, regardless of type.

Tom's point was that we spend the first half of our story discovering who the character is. From there, we spend the rest of the story ensuring that our character hews to that portrait.

My point is that we may only know the truth of who that character is and what she is about by writing through to the end. We may also only discover what our book is and what it's about by writing to the end. This is true whether we write fiction or nonfiction and whatever our theme, subject or genre.

Why stifle the creative process by refusing to surrender unconditionally to our book's unfoldment? Why rein in our book's infinite potential by insisting that at a certain point in a draft, everything of significance is fixed for all time?

When I was writing *The StarQuest,* I had a fairly clear idea of how one of my antagonists would meet her downfall in the final scenes. At least, I thought I did.

Then, on my final day's work on that initial draft, as I was letting the penultimate scene write itself, something unanticipated happened: Instead of the ugly death I was expecting for her, this villain had a profoundly redemptive experience that, within a few lines, had transformed her into a positive force for continuing good.

I was stunned.

In that moment, I had two choices: I could follow Tom's advice and refuse my villain her redemption, or I could surrender to the higher imperative of both the character and the story and surrender to the magic. I chose the latter, not only because I believe my books, stories and characters are smarter than I am, but because this character's transformation supported what I had begun to recognize as one of the book's central themes and it achieved it in ways that I would have been hard-pressed to consciously manufacture.

Even *Birthing Your Book* took on a different trajectory and structure than I had expected, something that occurred in the writing of it, not through any intervention of my logical mind. The more I wrote, the more I began to understand what the book was about — for me as well as for you. I have had similar experiences with all my books.

Unlike Tom, I say: Give your characters and books absolute freedom through the entire first draft and, if necessary, beyond. Let your characters be as inconsistent and mercurial as they want to be. Let you book veer off in a completely different direction partway through if that is what it needs to do.

Only by allowing your book that unconditional freedom in your early drafts can you learn what it is truly about and can you be true to its essence. After all, it is the book's story you are telling, not your own.

Let your first draft be that imperfect, muddled journey of discovery. You might, as I did in *The StarQuest,* only discover something of major significance on the final pages of the draft. That's okay. Use your next draft to bring consistency to the aspects and elements you now know more completely. Or you might discover, as I did with my *StarQuest* antagonist, that you wrote the character consistently without realizing it, and few if any alterations are needed.

Remember whose book you are writing…and get out of the way.

EXPLORATIONS

Ask yourself these questions and don't think about the answers. Let them emerge freely and honestly…on the Muse Stream, where appropriate:
- How can I better trust my books and, where relevant, their characters, to reveal themselves to me…in their fashion and time, not in mine?
- How can I stop trying to control my books into perfection and, instead, let them emerge organically?
- How can I better surrender to the magic out of which all creativity is birthed?
- How can I trust that my books know themselves better than I do?
- How can I let myself be surprised?
- What steps can I take today to start trusting more completely and surrendering more fully?

To Outline or Not to Outline?

One of the questions I am asked most often involves outlines. Do I or don't I?

I don't. At least not consciously on the page.

For me, the outline is an intellectual exercise that constrains my creative flow and throws mud into the sparkling waters of my Muse Stream. Worse, it places me in the driver's seat of a journey that I know myself to be ill-equipped to navigate on my own.

As I say repeatedly through these pages, your book knows itself better than you do…better than you ever will. Trying to bypass that innate wisdom and, instead, working at thinking your book out ahead of time threatens to strip it of all magic and serendipity, risks muzzling its potential…and yours.

Put another way, your book is a voyage of discovery and rediscovery — for you as much as for your reader. Such explorations thrive best when they are freed of preconceptions and unencumbered by rigid itineraries.

When *New York Times* bestselling author J.A. Jance admitted to me on my radio show that she has not outlined any of her fifty-plus books, I was stunned. Surely, I thought, if any literary form were to require an outline, it would be something as structured and plot-driven as mystery. Not for Jance. She begins each new book with a dead body and then, with neither outline nor advance notion of plot or outcome, writes her way to whodunnit and why. Stephen King's attitude is similar: "I distrust plot," he has said. "I do [it] as infrequently as possible."

I have outlined none of my books — not my novels, not my books on writing, not my memoir. To the dismay of many screenwriters, I have not even outlined my screenplays. Rather, I have relied on an intuitive knowingness — about what to write and when to write it and, later in the process, about how to shape, structure, revise, hone and polish it through to its final draft. My intuition has never let me down.

If the Muse Stream is about trust, it's also about intuition. It's about recognizing that, at deep levels, we already know the book we have been called on to write. It's about listening to the inherent wisdom and inner vision that resides in those deep places. It's about trusting that wisdom and vision, unconditionally.

When we allow ourselves to surrender to that intuitive process, we don't need outlines. We need only one word and then the next and then the next, in the moment-to-moment unveiling that is the gift of the Muse Stream.

That doesn't make outlining wrong. There are no absolutes in creativity — no absolute rights and no absolute wrongs, as my Rule #1 for Birthing Your Book points out. Your responsibility as writer-creator is to be open to whichever tools, techniques, processes, rhythms and routines reveal themselves to you and to adopt those that work best for you. It's also your responsibility to not get stuck in any of them. Remember that what works for you today on one draft or project might not be appropriate tomorrow on another (Book-Birthing Rule #2).

The key in this as in all things is to serve the book not our perceived need to control it, which, too often, is what an outline ends up being about.

If you feel you must outline, don't treat the result as gospel. View it instead as a general trajectory from which you are free to stray — randomly, wildly, illogically and frequently. Consider, too, outlining on the Muse Stream, which is more an exercise in brainstorming than in point-by-point outlining. How? Go nonlinear with techniques such as free association or mind mapping and let the exercise be one of expansion rather than constriction, of revelation rather than rote. Or plant a Word Tree, using the exercise in the next chapter.

The Word Tree

A Word Tree[2] is a nonlinear type of outline designed to open your mind to fresh ideas and new possibilities. Here's how to plant your own.

In the center of a large piece of blank, unlined paper, print "My Book" and draw a circle around it. This is the trunk of your Word Tree. If you are working on a particular aspect of your book or know your book's title, you can use that as your Word Tree's trunk.

Now, without stopping to think, analyze, criticize or judge, write the first word or phrase that leaps to mind, whether or not it's logically connected to "My Book."

Circle your new word, link it with a line to "My Book" and continue — by quickly writing, circling and linking the words triggered by each new association.

See each circled word or phrase as a leaf and each connecting line as a branch in this Word Tree you are growing.

Continue free-associating in this way until you feel complete with a particular branch. Then, either return to "My Book" or begin a new branch from any word or phrase you have already jotted down. Keep going for five, ten or fifteen minutes or longer, until you have a sense that your Word Tree has grown to maturity.

Once your Word Tree is complete, scan the page — again, not with your critical or analytical mind. Do it instead from that same open, intuitive, free-flowing place you used in "Birthing Your Book: A Meditative Journey" (Section 3).

As you do, let a word or phrase float up into your awareness from your unconscious. It could be a word or phrase that jumps out at you from the Word Tree, or it could be something else altogether. Whatever it is, jot it down, and let it be the kickoff to an experience in writing on the Muse Stream.

Now, write nonstop for twenty to thirty minutes, setting a timer should that be helpful. Remember to write nonstop on the Muse Stream, without pausing to correct spelling, punctuation or grammar or to hunt for the

---

[2] The Word Tree is based on the clustering technique developed and popularized by Gabriele Lusser Rico in her landmark book, *Writing the Natural Way* (Tarcher/Penguin, 1983, 2002).

"right" word. Remember, too, that if you feel stuck, you can use the repetition, free association or Jabberwocky-nonsense tips in "Help! I'm Stuck!" (Section 2) to reinitiate the flow.

When your time is up, set your writing aside for at least an hour. Use that time to take a walk or to do something else unrelated to your book. Then, when you feel able to look at what you have written uncritically and without judgment, read it — with an open heart and mind — and see what it tells you about your book, yourself or both. While this exercise is not designed to produce direct content for your book, it may.

If you feel unable to read what you have written without judgment, revisit the "Let Judgment Go" meditation in Section 5.

Return to this exercise any time you feel the need for a kickstart. "Fifty Keys to Your Book's Conception and Creation" (Section 3) can also offer up an effective inspirational boost.

Word Pictures

Writing a book is like painting a picture crafted with words not colors, words that must evoke entire worlds for your reader…worlds of people, worlds of places, worlds of objects, worlds of emotions. As such, it is your job as author-creator to paint into your word pictures the details and specifics that will bring those worlds alive, that will insert your reader more fully into those worlds, that will give your reader an individual experience of those worlds.

This is as true in nonfiction as it is in fiction. Think memoir, biography, autobiography and history: These all tell stories. But every book tells a story of some sort, and all stories benefit from the evocative word pictures that specifics and examples can supply.

As you describe your people and places, subjects and objects, use all your senses — spiritual as well as physical — to make them real for your readers. What are the colors — of eyes, cars, sunsets, buildings, moods? Are there original ways you can express those colors? With metaphor? From a different point of view? From a child's perspective?

Name your dogs, birds, towns, streets, characters.

What's the model of the car? The year? Is the interior cloth or leather? New-looking or worn? Pristine or littered with greasy McDonald's cartons?

Describe foods, settings, backgrounds.

What are the smells and sounds? The textures? The memories they evoke? The emotions they trigger?

Open to new ways of relating these to your reader. What do they remind you of? Who do they remind you of?

In nonfiction, can you give examples or tell stories that help illustrate what you are trying to say? Look for ways to bring those stories and examples to life.

As in all aspects of your writing, stay in balance. Over-description and mega-detail can be as off-putting as not enough. Allow what you paint to most resemble an Impressionist painting — sketching in enough color and detail to allow your readers to "connect the dots," but not so hyper-real that it overwhelms them.

Try This

As you move through your day — at home, at work, on errands or at play — pay attention to the specifics of what you see and experience. Note colors, shapes, sizes and textures. Note scratches, markings and other details. Note styles, brands, classes and breeds. Pinpoint tastes and smells. Be aware of your emotional responses and of the memories and associations evoked by what you are seeing and experiencing. If there are particular sights, sounds, places or experiences around you that are relevant to your book, take special notice of those, making notes and snapping photos if that helps you remember them.

Know Your World

Discover as much as you can about the worlds you're writing about, including your settings and characters (or subjects, if you're writing memoir, autobiography or biography).

With people, know not only their physical attributes but their secrets and dreams. Know not only the color of their eyes but the quality of the fire behind those eyes. Know what happened in their lives before you entered the scene, before their recorded story begins. Know what shaped them and still shapes them, what excites them, what scares them. Know them as well as — better, perhaps, than — you know yourself and, in that knowing, they will leap off the page with full humanity.

With places, know not only how they look but how they feel. Know not only what's visible but what's invisible. Know what's ordinary and extraordinary about them. Use all your senses to discover and describe their sounds, smells and textures. Their essence and spirit. Their character. Do the same with objects of significance to your story and book.

Here are six ways to deepen your knowledge of the worlds of your book and story.

1. Visualization

Close your eyes and get into a meditative space. Envision yourself in a safe, creative place and let your character or characters take shape.

Have them guide you through their day, their home, their life. Notice how they dress, how they wear their hair, how they walk, how they talk. Let them show you who they are and how they live. Let them show you who they were and where they came from. Let them show you who they will be and how they expect to get there. Watch them relate to others — to people they love and respect and to people they hate and fear. See them as they experience joy and pain. Eavesdrop on them in an intimate moment. Witness their response to crisis, to shock, to betrayal.

With settings, see yourself walking or driving through them, floating above them, looking up from beneath them. How else can you view them? Note the differences each perspective offers you.

Explore not only the seen but the unseen, the past and possible future as well as the present. Visit the attractive and desirable, but also check out the unattractive and squalid. Explore and experience it all, calling on all your senses, physical as well as spiritual and intuitive.

2. Meditative Dialogue

Just as you did in "Talk to Your Book" (Section 5), get into a meditative space and enter into a written conversation — this time with your characters. Ask questions and wait for answers. Let your characters tell you who and what they are...how they are feeling and why. You can do the same with place and with animals...even with inanimate objects. For they, too, can be living, sentient characters in your story.

After a few drafts of *The MoonQuest*, three of my four main characters didn't feel fully formed. I dialogued with each of them in turn and discovered things I hadn't known, including some uncomfortable things I didn't think I wanted to know, even as they proved integral to the story. Those dialogues became scenes that merged seamlessly into the narrative, as if the book had been waiting for them...and for me.

3. Imagery

Give your senses free rein. Ask not only what your character or nonfiction subject looks like, but what he sounds like, what she smells like, what his skin feels like. If your character were a taste or a flavor, what would that be? If your character were an animal or a bird, which animal or bird would she be? If he were a color or shape, which would he be?

Use imagery, too, to deepen your sense of place, describing it in ways that call not only on sight, sound, taste, touch and smell but on all sensory possibilities, including the numinous and otherworldly.

Remember to use your intuitive and visionary abilities — we all have them — to tune in to the story of his life, the life of her story...to tune in to the spirit and essence of each place...to the spirit and essence of your book.

These same tools can help you with the flora and fauna of your story, as well as with objects appearing in the foreground and background.

Need some help with your imagery? Experiment with and adapt the "Inside Your Book" meditation (Section 5) for this purpose.

4. Point Of View

Write as your character, in first person and on the Muse Stream, from his or her point of view. For example, "My name is..." or "I love to..." or "When I look in the mirror, I see..." Or write on the Muse Stream in third person using your character's name as a key word. If you don't yet know her name, write "This character's name is..." You can also write on the Muse

Stream from any attribute or attributes. For example, "Joanne's hair is…" or "Jack's favorite pastime is…" or "When Frieda meets a new person, she…"

To learn more about how your characters relate to their family, friends and environment, write about them from the point of view of other characters in the book. Write about them, too, from the perspective of the places they work, visit or inhabit.

If your objects or settings have character-like significance, explore them in a similar fashion. "I am John's house. When he's home, I…" "I am the New York of Janet and her story. I…" Write about the places from the point of view of different characters for a fuller sense of their depth and relevance.

5. Observation

Next time you're out, watch the people around you. What can you discern about them and about their lives from simple actions, behaviors and physical characteristics? Note how they sit, stand and walk, how they hold themselves. Be aware how they relate to others, both people they appear to know and strangers. Notice not only what they're wearing but how they're wearing it. Pay attention to what is being revealed; pay attention, too, to what might be being concealed.

Don't be embarrassed to eavesdrop. All writers are closet (or not-so-closet) voyeurs. Listen to what the people around you are saying and how they're saying it. Listen for rhythms of speech. Correlate what they're saying with their actions and body language and be aware of inconsistencies.

As you watch and listen to people in the "real" world, also be aware of their environment. How would you describe what you're seeing? Notice everything and be in the moment with everything you experience, employing all your senses — visionary as well as physical.

How can you apply what you are seeing and hearing to the subjects, objects and settings in the worlds of your book, nonfiction as well as fiction?

6. Lists

Create a detailed checklist of attributes and characteristics for your people and places or use the ones I have created in the next two chapters. Then, from a place of openness and surrender, run through each attribute and characteristic and allow its specifics to emerge…easily. As in all your writing, go with first thoughts and don't second-guess what emerges, however odd it might seem. Experiment by writing on the Muse Stream from any responses you get.

EXPLORATIONS

Ask yourself these questions and don't think about the answers. Let them emerge freely and honestly…on the Muse Stream, where appropriate:
- Which of my book's characters or settings come across as flat and one-dimensional, more cardboard-cutout than real?
- What can I add to my book that will bring its subjects, objects and settings to life for my readers?
- How can I create and populate worlds that are as real to my readers as they are to me?

Populating the Worlds of Your Book

From a place of openness and surrender, run through each attribute in the list and allow your character to tell you how it applies to him or her. Don't think about the answer; let it come easily, spontaneously. Let the character also show you how these attributes play out in his or her life.

Feel free to revise the list and to adapt it to your own needs, eliminating characteristics that aren't relevant and adding ones better tailored to your story.

Remember: Many of these attributes may never make it directly into your book. They will, however, inform and enrich your storytelling.

- First word or phrase that leaps to mind as you think of this character
- Name / Nickname
- Age (actual or approximate)
- Age this person acts or wishes s/he were
- Height / Weight / Body Type / Posture
- Nationality
- Complexion
- Hair (color, style, length) / Facial hair
- Eyes (shape, color)
- Quality of vision / Glasses? Contacts?
- Scars / Attitude toward scars
- Unusual physical characteristics
- Gait (how this person walks)
- Voice / Manner (soft? grating? blustery?)
- Favorite expression
- Favorite color
- Unusual traits, mannerisms
- Eccentricities / Odd habits
- Fears / Phobias
- Maturity level

- Clothing (style, fabric, age, condition)
- Cellphone (age, style, brand, condition)
- Car or other vehicle (age, style, model, condition)
- Profession / Employment
- Hobbies / Interests
- Schooling
- Unusual skills
- Greatest wish / desire
- Best dream already fulfilled
- Greatest regret
- Worst nightmare
- Punctuality (never/always late/early/on time)
- Allergies
- Favorite foods/cuisine, snacks, alcoholic/nonalcoholic drinks
- Unusual foods, drinks
- How s/he takes coffee, tea and/or other regular beverage
- Favorite restaurant, bar
- Preferred music, reading, art, films, TV, etc.
- Favorite artist, musician, author, actor, director
- Pets
- Sexual orientation
- Marital/relationship status
- Parents' names, ages
- Children's names, ages
- Siblings' names, ages
- Best friend's name, age
- Pets' names, ages
- Relationship with and/or attitude toward men, women, children, pets
- Relationship with and/or attitude toward family, self
- Your random thought about this character

Painting the Worlds of Your Book

Use this checklist to flesh out your sense of the places that show up in your book — fiction or nonfiction. In fiction, don't overthink or try to figure what each attribute would be for each setting. Rather, get meditative and intuit the answers, trusting your first response.

Not every item will apply to every place in your book, nor could any list ever be exhaustive. Use what is relevant and discard the rest. Take notes if you choose, or simply let the list rekindle your imagination.

LOCATION
- General (region, city, town, etc.)
- Specific (street, road, etc.)

PACE OF LIFE
- Hurried / Frenzied?
- Leisurely / Lazy / Slow?
- Urban? Rural?

TIME
- Time of year / Season / Date (specific or approximate)
- Time / Time of day

WEATHER & CLIMATE
- Temperature
- Aridity / Humidity
- Type, quantity, quality of precipitation, wind, cloud, sun, fog
- Relevant sights, sounds, smells

EXTERIORS — GENERAL TOPOGRAPHY
- Altitude
- Flat? Rolling? Hilly? Mountainous?
- Rocks, cliffs
- Barren? Lush? Desert?

- Bodies of water: Ocean, river, lake, stream, swamp, marsh, puddles
- Relevant sights, colors, sounds, smells, textures

EXTERIORS — IMMEDIATE NATURAL ENVIRONMENT
- Place where the scene takes place
- Neighboring area
- Middle- / Long-distance views
- Trees, flowers, grasses, shrubs, other plants/plantings
- Natural growth? / Planted by humans? When?
- Lushness / Sparseness / Health
- Soil color, type, moisture/dryness
- Relevant sights, colors, sounds, smells, textures

EXTERIORS — BUILT ENVIRONMENT
- Age, condition
- Building(s) where the scene takes place
- Neighboring/nearby structures
- Relationship between structures
- Roads, sidewalks, pavement
- Street architecture (benches, lampposts, trashcans)
- Signs
- Middle- / Long-distance views
- Relevant colors, sounds, smells, textures

EXTERIORS — VEHICLES
- Cars, motorcycles, bicycles
- Buses, trucks, vans
- Farm/industrial vehicles
- Pushcarts, shopping carts, wheelbarrows
- Baby carriages/strollers
- Animal-drawn vehicles
- Other vehicles
- Age, condition
- Visible drivers, passengers (See also "People & Animals")
- Relevant sights, colors, sounds, smells, textures

INTERIORS — VEHICLES
- Type, age, condition
- Drivers, passengers (See also "People & Animals")
- Relevant sights, colors, sounds, smells, textures

INTERIORS — INDOOR ENVIRONMENT
- General look, style, state, condition, age
- Furnishings, floor coverings
- Wall hangings, art / Knickknacks
- Light (quality, source)
- Windows, window coverings
- Plants, flowers
- Food, drink
- Electronics (computers, TVs, stereos, telephones)
- Relevant sights, colors, sounds, smells, textures

INTERIOR — INDOOR CLIMATE
- Comfortable? Uncomfortable? How?
- Aridity / Humidity / Temperature
- Relevant sights, colors, sounds, smells

PEOPLE & ANIMALS
See also "Populating the Worlds of Your Book"
- Ages
- Types
- Sizes
- Activities

MISCELLANEOUS
- General atmosphere, ambience
- Normal v. unusual
- Visible v. invisible
- Public v. secret
- Numinous/supernatural/sacred

DOMINANT SENSORY STIMULI
- Sights
- Colors
- Tastes
- Smells
- Sounds
- Textures
- Spirit

Secondary & Subtle Sensory Stimuli
- Sights
- Colors
- Tastes
- Smells
- Sounds
- Textures
- Spirit

Driven to Distraction?

Between the real demands of everyday life, the marketing demands that now face all writers and the ambivalence many of us can sometimes feel about the act of writing, it's a wonder that any words find their way onto anyone's page. What about you? Do any of these "I have to's" sound familiar?

Before I can write…
- I have to check my email or voicemail or Facebook or Google+ or Twitter or Tumblr or Pinterest or Instagram or…
- I have to take or make this one phone call or respond to this one text message, Facebook post or tweet.
- I have to watch this one YouTube video.
- I have to eat (I can't write on an empty stomach) or fuel myself with caffeine (I have to make a fresh pot of tea or coffee).
- I have to start or finish just one more game on my phone or computer.
- I have to walk the dog…or water the plants…or weed the garden…or clean the litter box…or…
- I have to scrub the bathroom floor…or vacuum…or wash the car…or…
- I have to do more research.

Before you do any of those things, read on for seven surefire tips to help you minimize distraction and limit procrastination.

1. Get Thee Offline

Keep all Internet and mobile-device distractions out of sight and earshot until after you have written. That means no social media and no email. In fact, don't open your web browser unless you write using a browser app. If you have a smartphone or data-equipped tablet, either switch it off altogether or put it in airplane mode. (Don't cheat by reenabling your device's wifi.)

2. Silence Is Golden

Don't answer your phone or check your voice mail. Don't look at incoming text messages or respond to them. To avoid temptation while you're writing, turn off all phone ringers and mute all notifiers (visual as well as audible) for email, social media, text messages and/or smartphone/tablet/computer apps. There shalt be no flashes, beeps or pings to disturb your focus. (You have already disabled your cell phone, right?)

3. No News Is Good News

Don't open your mail. Don't check your mailbox for mail. Don't open the morning paper. Don't check to see if it has arrived. Don't check online news sites. (You have closed your browser. Remember?) Keep the TV off. Stay away from YouTube. Only listen to the radio if it's all-music…and only if it's the type of music that inspires rather than distracts.

4. Post No Bills

When paying bills or balancing your checkbook is more attractive than writing, you know you're in trouble. Don't open your checkbook to pay bills or visit your online banking site or your bank's mobile app. Don't visit any website or mobile app. (You have closed your browser and gone offline with your phone and tablet, right?)

5. To Everything There Is A Season

This is not the season to start that book you have been meaning to read or to catch up on your DVR'd TV shows or favorite Netflix series. Nor is it the season to pick up that book you're a few pages from finishing or that magazine article you're nearly done with. It's the season to write.

6. Cleanliness May Be Next To Godliness…But Creativity Is Godly

Stay away from sponges, mops, vacuum cleaners, feather dusters and cleaning rags. Don't go near the Windex or all-purpose cleaner. Ignore the dishes piling up in your kitchen sink. If your toilet or cat's litter box is revolting, they can remain revolting for a few hours longer. There is only one thing to do and you know what it is: Write, right?

7. Axe The Xbox

Keep all gaming devices switched off. Avoid all computer, tablet and smartphone games. Make the next game played your reward for having met your writing goals.

In short: Don't do *anything* unrelated to writing. Now is the time to write!

Try This

If keeping distractions at bay has proven impossible, keep pen and paper or your laptop or tablet by your bed, and don't get out of bed until you have written. That's how I got through the initial third of my first drafts of both *The MoonQuest* and *The StarQuest*.

With *The MoonQuest*, I was so stressed by the notion of surrendering to the story (even though I was already teaching the philosophy) that I stayed in bed until I had achieved my morning's writing goal.

With *The StarQuest*, I also stayed in bed, but that was because those were my only stress-free, distraction-free, exhaustion-free moments of the day. Writing also set a positive tone for the hours ahead, filled as they were with a physically demanding, spiritually stifling job.

Another benefit of making writing your first assignment of the day (other than getting it done) is that you don't waste time through the rest of your day collecting meaningless distractions to avoid having to write.

Now Try This

Don't turn the page. Don't walk away. Don't think. Pick up your pen or touch your fingers to the keyboard. Start writing. *Now.*

Read to Write, Read to Live

Writing a book is most often a solitary act, one that can pull us out of the maelstrom of daily living and into a monastic place of creative retreat. When you're in the midst of birthing a book — and even when you're not — it's important to be part of the shared world of creation and imagination inhabited by your fellow authors. Take time to read as much good writing as you can, regardless of form, medium or genre. Here's why…

1. Expansion

Reading, along with all the arts, expands us as human beings, as conscious beings and as writers. Whether you spend time in your own genre or another, you will deepen your knowledge of the human experience, including your own, and connect with both the heart of creation and the creator of heart and art.

2. Craft

Osmosis is one of the most powerful learning tools available to the human heart and mind. When we read great writing, we absorb the author's craft and technique. We sense at a deep level what works and what doesn't. Without having to know or understand how or why, without needing to analyze or parse, the power of the words we read finds its way into our writing.

You won't be copying. You will be absorbing, filtering and adapting. You will be learning — in the easiest and most fun way imaginable: by doing nothing other than enjoying another's words.

Once again, form and genre don't matter. Topic doesn't matter. What matters is that you read good writing by accomplished authors.

3. Stress-Reduction And Creativity Enhancement

Reading, say researchers at Britain's University of Sussex, is one of the best ways to relax and lower stress levels — more effective than listening to music, drinking tea or coffee, going for a walk or playing video games. The university's 2009 study suggests that even six minutes of silent reading can cut your stress by sixty-eight percent, slowing your heart rate and easing heart and muscle tension. According to cognitive neuropsychologist Dr. David Lewis, who conducted the study, "Losing yourself in a book is the ultimate relaxation." Reading, he notes, stimulates your creativity and places you in what is essentially an altered state of consciousness. "This is more than merely a distraction," Lewis insists, "but an active engaging of the imagination."

4. Blatant Self-Interest

Do you want to be read? Do you want your book to find an audience? If you as a writer aren't reading, what sort of example are you setting for your potential readers?

The creative/literary community is not a one-way delivery system. It's a bustling marketplace of ideas and concepts where readers not only learn and grow from writers, but where writers learn and grow from readers and from each other. If we write, in part, to be heard, then we must also be prepared to listen.

Again, genre and subject are less important than engagement, than opening a book — any book — and surrendering to the words and imaginings of a fellow artist.

Explorations

Ask yourself these questions and don't think about the answers. Let them emerge freely and honestly…on the Muse Stream, where appropriate:
- Why is reading important to me?
- Which books and authors have influenced the book I'm writing? My writing in general? My life? How has that influence expressed itself?
- Which books and authors have inspired me? In what ways?

If you aren't reading, visit your nearest bookseller or public library or browse your favorite online bookstore and discover the words and worlds that are waiting for you on their real or virtual shelves. Step beyond the walls of your creative enterprise and engage.

- *If the world of storytellers and storytelling is important to you — as both reader and writer — discover what life would be like if that world vanished. That's the premise of* The MoonQuest, *the first volume of my Q'ntana fantasy trilogy.*

7. Vision

First you stumble, then you fall
You reach out and you fly
There isn't anything that you can't do
Rita MacNeil, singer/songwriter

If I create from the heart, nearly everything works;
if I create from the head, almost nothing.
Marc Chagall, artist

What's Your Vision for Your Book?

Do you have a vision for your book? What purpose do you hope it will serve in your life and in the lives of those who ultimately read it? Perhaps you already know. Perhaps you don't. In either case, a vision statement can help.

If you don't yet have a conscious vision, crafting a vision statement will bring your book's aim and intention into clearer focus. If you do, invoking your vision statement before you sit down to work with your book will keep you aligned with its energy, theme and focus through the entire process of conception, creation, revision and release.

The vision statements I have created for my books have often served as part of my gear-change from the outer to the inner, from mind-focus to Muse-focus, and have ensured that all I wrote hewed as closely as possible to the book's true essence. They have also reminded me of my aim in writing the books once post-publication reviews and comments start coming in.

A vision statement can be as brief as a sentence or two or as long as a page. It can speak in broad terms about your role as writer or in more specific terms about your book's purpose. Nor are vision statements fixed for all time. As your book progresses and you mature through the writing of it, you may feel called to refine your vision statement to match your new insights and awareness.

What's your vision for your book? Don't think about it. Feel it. And when you start to feel it, write it. It doesn't have to make sense. Just let it be what it is.

On the next pages you will find three vision statements I have created plus "Vision Quest," a guided meditation that can help you both connect with your vision for your book and create a vision statement of your own. The exercise that follows "Finding the 'Vision' in Revision" (Section 8) offers another way to put your vision for your book into words.

My Vision Statement for *The Voice of the Muse*

The Voice of the Muse: Answering the Call to Write is about freedom — freedom to grow, freedom to create, freedom to write. Through a dynamic blend of motivational essays, inspiring meditations and practical exercises, it nourishes, nurtures and reassures its readers, inspiring them to open their hearts, expand their minds and experience, with ease, a full, creative life.

My Vision Statement for *Acts of Surrender*

Acts of Surrender is an exploration for me and an inspiration for its readers.

It's designed to open readers to the possibilities of freedom in their own lives and to the gifts of surrender.

It's about a life not lived without fear but in spite of fear, a life lived in surrender to a higher imperative, a life lived as The Fool in the tarot lives his life: in faith, and trusting (not always with evidence) that all is good, all is safe, all is provided for and all is one.

As I write, I let my stories reveal their innate teachings through the telling of them.

My job is to keep interpretation to a minimum.

My job is to recount and relate, to reveal and recapitulate, to walk the earth naked once more, clothed only in the truths that have revealed themselves to me through the living of them.

I open my heart to this story, my story, more baldly and boldly told than through any fantasy parable, as powerful as such telling can be and is.

I open my heart and reveal my vulnerabilities and fears (and, yes, revel in them) so that others may feel free to reveal, revel in and move through theirs.

Acts of Surrender: A Writer's Memoir is about the consciousness of freedom through surrender, awakening and revealing itself in the hearts of all those it touches.

My Vision Statement for the *Q'ntana* Screenplays and Stage Musicals

These stories have always been bigger than me — from the moment the first one insisted itself onto the page, then as a series of novels and now as their screenwriter and librettist. These are stories that have so long been such a part of my life that it's as though they live deep within my cells. I am every one of their characters, villain as much as hero, and have lived each of their joys, triumphs, disappointments, betrayals and disasters. For decades, I have watched their themes play out in the world around me, just as I have experienced them play out in my own life…and not always comfortably. In the end, I am more than the storyteller. I am the story.

Vision Quest: A Guided Meditation

ALLOW AT LEAST 30 MINUTES TO COMPLETE THIS MEDITATION
AND FOR THE WRITING THAT FLOWS FROM IT.

Relax. Close your eyes. Let your hands fall to your lap if you're sitting, to your abdomen if you're lying down. Breathe…deeply…in and out…in and out…in and out.

If you are setting off on this journey any later than first thing in the morning, run back over your day on fast-forward, and every time you get to something that was harsh or jarring, be it a thought, word or action — yours or someone else's — breathe in deeply and blow it out. As fully and noisily as you dare. As many times as you need to. Just blow it out.

And any moment that was particularly wonderful, breathe it in deeply and reconnect with the energy of that.

Continue to breathe, deeply, and focus on your eyes. If you wear glasses or contacts, imagine, for a moment, perfect vision without them. Imagine unassisted clarity without correction.

Breathe into that.

See white light around your eyes and your third eye, that chakra or energy center that lies between your eyebrows and above the bridge of your nose. See that white light cleaning, clearing and cleansing any blurriness, fuzziness, distortion. Feel all veils being pulled away, one by one by one by one. And as each veil dissolves, your vision becomes clearer and clearer and clearer.

Now, without removing all your attention from your eyes, move some of your focus to your heart. Be aware of the veils that surround your heart, whatever form they take.

Just be aware of them. Don't judge them.

Now, taking a deep breath, let the outermost veil fall away. Feel it fall away and dissolve. And when you breathe in again, notice that your heart feels lighter and freer and clearer.

And as you breathe in again, another veil falls away. And another. And another.

Feel how much lighter your heart feels, how much freer your heart feels. It's okay if it feels a bit scary. Just feel what you feel. Know that you are safe.

Keep breathing and feel yourself grow lighter and freer, lighter and freer, as you move closer to the heart of the matter and closer to who you are as the writer and author you are.

And what a wondrous place that is.

Once more, breathe in, and if there is another veil there, breathe it away. And the next. And the next. And the next, until all that remains is a brilliant light, no longer veiled and dimmed, in your heart. Breathe into that and feel it.

Now, let the light from your eyes and the light from your heart connect in a ring of light that circulates energy from eyes to heart and around again. Either clockwise or counterclockwise. It doesn't matter. Whichever way it happens is perfect for you. However the light moves for you, allow yourself to sense it, to feel it. Your vision and your heart as one.

Now, see a second ring of light, moving in the opposite direction from the first, this time connecting your heart to the hands resting on your lap or abdomen. Again, be aware of the circular motion of this circulating energy. Around and around. A constant and consistent river of radiance.

Connect the two rings and you now have figure eight or infinity symbol within you, as this inner light arcs from eyes to heart…heart to hands…hands to heart…heart back to eyes. And again. And again. And again, creating an infinite, luminous flow with your heart as its center.

As the energy circulates through that figure eight, be aware of the light pulsing in the topmost tips of your fingers, the hands with which you create, the hands that form part of the channel that brings your worlds into reality. Perhaps you feel the pulsing. Perhaps you don't. Whatever you feel physically, know that the energy is there, the light is there. The creative power is there — in your fingers, in your hands, in your eyes and in your heart, as the flow continues.

Sit with that flow for a few moments, feeling yourself immersed in its river of light and in the creative power that is moving through you.

Now, move your focus away from the infinity symbol and back to your eyes, your heart and your hands. Let a beam of light radiate out from your eyes, another beam of light from your heart and a third beam of light from your hands — all meeting at a point in front of you, in front of your heart.

That point in front of you, connected to you by all that light, is your work as a writer…is your book, is the book that has called to you. The book you are now writing or, if you have not yet started, the book you will soon be writing.

So your book stands separate from you but connected to you, in that space where all the beams of light meet in front of you, in front of your heart. There is your writing. There is your book.

I'm going to ask you some questions about your book. I want you to allow the first answer that comes to mind to be the answer, even if it seems to make no sense in the moment. And I want you to know that you will remember it long enough to put it on paper if that's where it needs to go.

So, focusing the beams of light that travel from your heart, eyes and hands and onto that writing space in front of you, onto that book in front of you…

- What is it that, deep inside of you, you want to convey through your book? First answer. No thinking about it. Let the answer come freely.
- What is it you want people to experience through your book? Again, go with whatever comes up first. Don't censor. Don't judge.
- What do you want people to experience of you through your book?
- What do you want people to experience of themselves through your book?

Open your eyes and note your answers to those questions, to whichever questions were answered.

Remember not to judge or analyze. Just record your experiences, the answers you have received.

Stay in a meditative space and, when you're finished, turn to a fresh sheet of paper. At the top of the page, write: "I, [your name], am a writer. Through my book [or the title of the book], I…"

From that opening, write on the Muse Stream, letting what follows be as long or as short as it needs to be.

When you're finished, sit quietly in the energy of that for a few minutes before reading it aloud. Feel free to revisit and revise this statement or series of statements as you and your book mature through its conception, creation, revision, completion and release.

- *My recording of a longer, two-part version of this meditative experience is included — along with ten other, equally inspiring tracks — on "The Voice of the Muse Companion: Guided Meditations for Writers." Look for it on Amazon, iTunes and Google Play and from other online music sellers.*

8. Revision

The most difficult thing in the world is to be simple.
　　Stanley Cortez, cinematographer

In any art…one of the deepest secrets of excellence is discernment.
　　Rex Stout, novelist

Reclaiming the "Vision" in Revision

We are accustomed to experiencing the editing process as a brutal, left-brain activity too often filled with violent and abusive language: It's about *forcing* the book to our will, *gagging*, *restraining* or *reining in* our characters, *hacking away* at our work or *hammering* our manuscript into shape. Yet when we treat our drafts with such disdain and disrespect, we are also demeaning and disrespecting ourselves as their author.

Instead of this harsh, aggressive approach, see the editing process as one of *re*vision, of revisiting your original vision for your book and putting all your heart, art and skill into aligning what's on paper with that vision.

As you move through draft after draft, see yourself as a jeweler, delicately etching your rough stone into the gem that reflects the vision your heart has conceived and received, then lovingly polishing it until you achieve the look and texture that you know it desires from you.

Your vision is the light force of your work, the life force of your work. It is the spirit that is its essence, the breath that keeps it alive. Your vision is your dream for your work, the expression of your intention. It is what guides it, drives it and propels it — from conception to completion and beyond. The more fully you are able to stay connected to that vision, however broadly or specifically you have drawn it, the more completely your finished book will remain true to that life force, that dream, that intention. And the truer you will be to the book that has called upon you to commit it to paper and breathe life into it.

Try This

Have you already crafted a vision statement for your book (Section 7)? If so, keep your vision statement handy as you revise your manuscript. If not, here's another opportunity to create one.

Your vision statement can be as simple as getting into a meditative space and writing on the Muse Stream from the phrase, "My vision for my book is…" or, perhaps more accurately, "My book's vision for me is…" (If you already have a title, insert it in place of "my book.")

Alternatively, allow your work to speak about itself, writing on the Muse Stream from one of the following phrases:
- I am [Your Name's book *or* Title of book]. I am about…
- I am [Your Name's book *or* Title of book]. I am here to…
- I am [Your Name's book *or* Title of book]. I have come into your life and into the lives of your readers to…
- I am [Your Name's book *or* Title of book]. Let me…

If a more guided approach would be helpful, return to the "Vision Quest" meditation in the previous section.

Whatever your choice, allow to come whatever comes, whether it speaks in metaphor, in general terms or with the most specific of detail. The length doesn't matter. The form and language don't matter. Your conscious mind's understanding of what you have written doesn't matter.

What matters is that, at some level, you and your book sing the same song and that that harmony supports you not only as you write but as you refine and enrich each draft.

Entering into the Spirit of Revision

Before you launch into revision, before you even open your manuscript in editing mode, revisit your vision statement. Do more than read it. Feel it. Embody it. Connect with it and, through it, connect with the essence of your book.

Where possible, read your vision statement aloud — with heart, power, confidence and intent. Thus empowered, the words of your vision statement will fuel and inspire you as you move through each draft and each revision, all the way through to the final draft.

Once you have revisited your vision, let the tips and techniques in this section guide you as you revisit and revise your work.

1. Talk To Your Book

Remember "Talk to Your Book" (Section 5)? Your conversations don't end the moment you complete your first draft. Continue to use that meditative-dialogue technique all the way through the revision process and your book will tell you what is missing from your manuscript and what needs refining. Listen with your heart and trust what you hear — in terms of your book's content, shape, theme, format, language and structure. Remember: Your book knows best, through every stage of your journey together.

2. Take Your Time

There's no rush. Let your manuscript sit quietly for a time before you launch into revision. That time could be a day, a week, a month or six months after you complete a draft. And it could be longer or shorter from one draft of your book to the next...and from one book to the next.

Even if a publisher or editor is pressuring you to finish a particular draft, don't panic. Remember that your book deserves you at your best, and your readers deserve the best from you. So give both yourself and your book the space and distance that allow you to approach your revisions heartfully, objectively and discerningly.

If you are feeling hypercritical and can't help but judge what you have written, wait until you feel able to read it from a place of wisdom and perception, not from one of self-criticism and self-doubt, and see #5, below.

3. Be True To Your Vision

As you revise your manuscript, hold your vision for your book (and your book's vision for you) in your heart and mind, and let that vision guide you as you make the changes that will keep you true to its spirit and essence.

4. Trust Your Inner Compass

As you become more adept as a writer, more in tune with your book and its vision and more in touch with your Muse, you will gain an intuitive knowingness of what works in your manuscript and what doesn't, without always being able to articulate why. That inner compass will direct you to the appropriate improvement or solution — again, often without explanation. Trust your intuition. It's the voice of your Muse, the voice of your book and the voice of your vision. It will never lead you astray.

5. Suspend Judgment

Heartful revision, which is the editing process I am advocating here, is about discernment, not judgment. We all judge ourselves and our work too harshly at times. Notice your judgment, but don't give in to it. And don't let it get in the way of your revisions and rewriting. If you need help suspending those judgmental tendencies we all carry, revisit the "Let Judgment Go" meditation (Section 5).

6. Accept That Language Is Not Perfect

As you revise, never hesitate to seek out more forceful and evocative ways to translate your vision onto the page. Remember, though, that translation is an art and that language can do no more than approximate emotion and experience. Think of the most evocative description you hope to include in your book and imagine trying to recreate that in words. Yes, you can come close. But whatever your mastery of the language, you will not recreate every nuance of your vision, emotion and experience. That's okay. Accept the creative perfection of that innate imperfection and…

7. Do Your Best

Do your best to write the words and paint the images that most accurately reflect your book, its stories and its vision. Do your best to commit that vision to paper. Do your best to polish, enrich and enliven your book so that it aligns with that vision. Do your best with each draft and, when it's time, declare it finished let it go.

8. Respect All Your Drafts

Revision is not about taking a broadax to your manuscript. It's about treating each draft as a necessary stage in its growth toward creative maturity…and yours. Just as you gently, sometimes firmly, guide your children toward the fulfillment of their unique destinies, guide your book with that same spirit of respect — for yourself as its creator as well as for your creation, which has its own vision and imperative.

No word you write is ever wasted. Each word is a necessary part of the journey toward a completed draft, and each draft is an integral part of the journey toward a completed book. Respect your initial draft. Respect all your drafts. Don't be a slave to them. Allow your work to evolve, and…

9. Be The Writer You Are

Each draft of your book will teach you, and from each draft you will mature in your art and your craft. Let each draft be what it needs to be. Let each draft be the foundation for your next. Let each book be what it needs to be. Let each book be the foundation for your next. Strive for excellence not perfection. Be the writer you are.

Mark David's Rules for Revision

More rules? More *non*-rules! That's because my first rule for revision is the same as my first rule for everything else, which is…

1. There Are No Rules

Of course, there aren't. There never are. In revision as in writing, there is no single right way that is guaranteed to work every time. There is only the way that works for you *today*. I emphasize "today" because what works for you in revising one draft or book may not always work on the next. So be open, be flexible and do whatever it takes to…

2. Trust Your Intuition

Don't rely only on the logical side of your brain to correct obvious errors. Use all your senses, especially your intuition, to *feel* if something works. Your intuition is the voice of your book. The more you trust it, the more it will alert you that something is not right and the more it will offer you effective ways to fix it.

3. Read Aloud

We are always more attuned to the rhythm and flow of our language when we read aloud. We often read more thoroughly when we read aloud. You will want to read your manuscript silently as well, of course. But particularly at the beginning and each time you make substantive changes, your voice will tell you where you have strayed off course.

4. Be Specific…But Not Too Specific

Now is the time to expand on descriptions that aren't specific enough. What make and color is the car? What does it smell like? What kind of flowers are in the bouquet? What shapes are the clouds? Is the grass clipped or unruly? Is it green or brown? This is also the time to dilute or delete unnecessary detail. Give your readers the specifics that will bring your story alive, but don't overwhelm them with superfluities.

5. Use Imagery...But Don't Overdo It

As you reread, revise and rewrite your manuscript, look for opportunities to increase or fine-tune your use of imagery. What do things smell and taste like? What do they sound like? What is their texture? Cross senses for more powerful imagery: Ask what the wind tastes like, what the earth sounds like...what someone's face feels like, what the town smells like, what your heartbeat looks like.

Connect your readers with the sensory power of your story, but don't overstimulate them. Imagery used wisely and judiciously will always enhance your book, regardless of its type or genre. Imagery used gratuitously will only disrupt your flow and bore your readers.

6. Paint Word Pictures That Draw On Related Images

For the title of this rule, I chose words like "paint," "pictures," "draw" and "images" to create and reinforce a particular idea. Would it have been as strong had I written, "Use word pictures that tap into related ideas"? You multiply the power of your imagery when you build on related images to describe something. When one image in the series breaks from the theme, you weaken your overall picture. As with any other tool, beware of excess.

7. Adopt The Rhythm Method

The rhythm, music and flow of your language show up not only in your choice of words and use of imagery but in how you structure your sentences. A series of short, simple sentences, for example, can build suspense or propel your reader forward. Longer, more complex sentences slow the reader down to a more leisurely pace.

As you read others' work, note how each author uses and varies his or her sentences. In your own work, does the type and length of your sentences support the scene you have written and the mood you seek to convey? Know the effect you want and use the rhythm of your language to achieve it.

Reading aloud, as I noted in Rule #3, can help you hear what is and is not working.

8. Use Powerful Nouns And Verbs

Adjectives and adverbs can act as crutches that prop up sickly nouns and weak verbs. Employ evocative verbs and descriptive nouns that stand on their own power and kick away those crutches. That doesn't mean you need to eliminate all adverbs and adjectives. These modifiers can, of course, be potent tools. But they will always be more potent when they are not only powerful in their own right but coupled with forceful verbs and nouns. To help you find the nouns and verbs (and adjectives and adverbs) that will enliven and strengthen your narrative...

9. Make Friends With A Thesaurus

Use a thesaurus (in revision, *not* while writing) to replace adjectives and adverbs with more expressive nouns and verbs. Use it, too, to find adverbs and adjectives that more eloquently and effectively reflect your intent. Words like "beautiful," "nice" and "interesting," for example, convey nothing to your reader. Find an adjective that more accurately states what it is you're trying to describe or express, or find a noun that eliminates the need for an adjective.

Don't rely solely on your writing program's built-in thesaurus. Both your local bookstore and the Internet are overflowing with more robust alternatives.

As with any friendship, don't abuse your relationship with your thesaurus. Use it as a tool, not as a crutch.

10. Keep It Simple

Be simple. Be direct. Avoid four- or five-syllable words when words of one or two syllables work as well. Avoid paragraph-long, James Joycean sentences when a series of shorter ones would be clearer and easier to follow. In simplicity lies power. Don't drown your reader in flowery excess. Don't show off. If you need help, revisit Revision Rule #9.

11. Cut The Fat

Are there words, phrases, sentences or scenes that detract from the essence of your book, that dilute your theme, that shroud your vision? Either cut them or rework them so that they strengthen the book and buttress your vision.

Have you used two or three words — or sentences — where one would do? Find ways to say more with less. Remember Revision Rule #10.

Have you overwhelmed your reader with imagery or description that doesn't move your book forward or that doesn't reveal character? Have you included explanations, illustrations, examples or arguments that repeat something you have already said? Cut the fat.

Look for words like "very," "actually," "really," "indeed," "just" and "quite." More often than not, actually, they are just filler and, indeed, really quite unnecessary.

12. Fill In The Gaps

You have written, "It was a beautiful day." What was beautiful about it? How did it make you feel? How did it make your character or subject feel? What did it smell like? What did it sound like? Describe it. Add flesh to your skeletons. Illuminate your scenes with detail and emotion.

13. Beware Unintended Meanings

Could your sentence be read two different ways with two different meanings? For example: "The mayor spoke about sex with Harriet." Rework it so that we know whether the topic was sex with Harriet or whether the mayor spoke with Harriet and the topic was sex.

Watch your punctuation and make certain that it supports your intention. Take this sentence: "Are you ready to eat, Grandma?" Once you remove the comma, Grandma is no longer being lunched. She's lunch.

14. Watch For Inconsistencies

Has Janet morphed into Jane partway through your manuscript? Does your description in one chapter fail to match your description of the same character, object or location in another chapter? It's easy for inconsistencies like these to creep into your manuscript, especially when you write rapidly on the Muse Stream. It's easy, too, to overlook them after multiple drafts and read-throughs. Be vigilant.

In my first draft of *The MoonQuest*, several characters renamed themselves partway through, sometimes multiple times. Through my various revisions of *Birthing Your Book*, I added, cut, moved and merged chapters and rules, affecting cross-references throughout the manuscript. Inconsistencies like these can be easy to miss on subsequent reads. Take note of changes as you make them if that will help you keep track when it comes time for revision.

15. Listen To Your Dialogue

Write dialogue that sounds natural and coherent not rambling or wooden. Listen to real people speaking — not to duplicate the content but to harmonize with the spirit — and always read your dialogue out loud. (Record and transcribe an unscripted conversation to see why you want your dialogue to be lifelike not true-life.)

Effective dialogue is rarely about long-stretches of expository monologue. Nor do you want to use dialogue to force-feed plot information to your readers. The former can be hard to read; the latter ends up feeling artificial.

Make sure that all your dialogue doesn't sound the same. Make sure that all your dialogue doesn't sound like you! Effective dialogue is true to each individual character's rhythm, style, cadence and vocabulary, not to yours.

If you're having trouble with your dialogue, spend meditative time in conversation with your characters. Listen as much to how they speak as to what they say.

16. Set Your Favorites Free

The sentence you love most, the description you consider unparalleled, the chapter you cannot bear to cut: These are your favorites, and you may have an unhealthy attachment to them. View them objectively, from a place of loving detachment. Look at them in light of your vision. Ask yourself if they serve the larger work. Ask your book whether they belong. If they don't, file them for later use in future projects.

17. Step Into Your Readers' Shoes

What have you not explained to your reader? Are there holes in your narrative that ought to be filled? Ask yourself the questions your readers will ask — and answer them.

18. Your Readers Are Smarter Than You Think

What have you over-explained? Are you telling readers too much? Your readers are smarter than you think. You don't need to explain everything for them, nor do you need to describe every detail of every situation or every moment of every day. Remember Revision Rule #11 and cut the fat.

19. You Are Certain To Make Changes You Will Regret

It's easy, during revision, to make changes in one draft that you regret in the next. To avoid losing your pre-corrected text, create a new document and printout for each draft. If you must make changes within a particular draft, keep the original text visible by enclosing your change in square brackets or by displaying it in a different font or color.

If your writing software allows you to revert to a previous draft, enable that feature. And if you have access to a backup system or service that saves multiple versions of a document, like Apple's Time Machine, do what it takes to retain access to those earlier drafts.

20. You Will Regret Missing Mistakes You Could Have Corrected

There will be errors you will miss. There will be errors that editors and proofreaders will miss. Regardless of the number of times you read your manuscript and have it read by others, including by professionals, typographical errors and other bloopers will slip through. When you discover them after publication, make note of them so that you can correct future editions. Then let them go.

21. Don't Obsess

Through every stage of your revision experience with your book, there will be infinite opportunities for you to obsess about one thing or another. Don't do it.

22. There Are No Rules

Each aspect of the writing process, including revision, is a creative act, and creativity is about experimentation and innovation. Find your own way…in your writing, in your rewriting and in your revision.

Trust Your Vision, Trust Your Book

It's March 1995, a chilly spring morning in rural Nova Scotia. With notepad on my lap, pen in hand and a fire crackling in the Kemac stove, I begin the day's work on my *MoonQuest* novel, grateful that this first draft is nearly finished. To my surprise, what emerges onto the page is not my usual third-person narrative. Instead, I find myself writing in the first person as Toshar, the story's main character.

It doesn't take me long to realize that Toshar's voice is the story's voice and that I will have to rewrite *The MoonQuest* from scratch, from his perspective. To do it, I know I will have to delete many scenes, add many new ones and subject those that survive to wholesale revision.

My old editor-self would have approached the task as an exercise in left-brain mechanics. My new Muse Stream-self recognizes the need for a more right-brain approach.

Instead of forcing *The MoonQuest* into this new, first-person form, I decide to treat the story as its own sentient entity and let it tell me what is necessary and what is expendable. Instead of trying to figure out which scenes to retain and which to cut, I choose to let the story find its own telling.

If all my experiences so far with *The MoonQuest* have helped me trust in the wisdom of the story, I now allow myself to trust it even more. The result? The rewrite and subsequent revisions stream out of me with an ease and speed I neither expected nor could have imagined.[3]

How did I do it? By following these basic Muse Stream precepts, as important in revision as they are in writing your first draft:

- Silence your critical and judgmental selves.
- Listen *for* the voice of your book. Listen *to* the voice of your book.
- Trust your book's innate wisdom and surrender to it, unconditionally.
- Get out of your book's way. Get out of your own way.
- Follow your intuition.
- Practice discernment.

Whether in writing, revision or life, these guidelines will never let you down. (See "Mark David's Rules for Living a Creative Life" in Section 10.)

---

[3] A dozen years later I would adapt *The MoonQuest* novel as a screenplay the same way.

9. Going Public

*The same number of people are going to hate it and like it,
so you might as well do the best you can and let it go.*
Frank Gehry, architect

*So long as you write what you wish to write,
that is all that matters; and whether it matters for ages
or only for hours, nobody can say.*
Virginia Woolf, novelist

Remember Your Vision Statement?

Your vision statement is not only a powerfully effective tool as you write and revise your book, it can also continue to serve you as you free your book out into the world — first in draft form for feedback and, later, once it's published.

Hold to this vision when you receive comments from friends and family and from your writers' group. Hold to it as well when agents and publishers respond to your work. Hold to it when your published book is reviewed. And hold to it whether it attracts praise or criticism.

Your vision, as embodied in and by your vision statement, will always keep you centered and aligned with the true heart of your work — whatever the world throws at you.

- *Have you crafted your vision statement yet? If not, return to Section 7 ("Vision") or try the exercise at the end of "Finding the 'Vision' in Revision" (Section 8).*

Author Support

Too often, we fail to recognize our creativity, can't see our talent, refuse to acknowledge our power. That's not surprising, given how solitary and insular book-writing can be, given how untrained so many people are in the words and actions that support another's creativity.

Groups can be a powerful antidote to that. By coming together with other writers, you have an opportunity to take all you have experienced and read in these pages and multiply it manyfold through the constructive support of others.

One way to forge creative connection and build creative support is by starting a Voice of the Muse Writers' Circle, a concept I initiated with *The Voice of the Muse: Answering the Call to Write*. It's easy: Share your passion, your commitment and *Birthing Your Book* with a few like-spirited authors and, voilà, you are part of a powerful vortex of motivation and inspiration.

Today, you don't even have to be in the same city or on the same continent to form a writers' group. Free services like Skype and Google Hangouts make it possible to connect with fellow writers nearly anywhere in the world. All it takes is a computer, a webcam, a high-speed Internet link, some basic tech knowhow and a rudimentary grasp of global time zones.

However you format your Voice of the Muse Writers' Circle, consider including the following elements, all geared toward keeping the experience a supportive and productive one for all:

1. CHECKING IN

When writing a book, mutual accountability can be a powerful motivator. Set aside time at every get-together for all members to share their book-birthing experiences. Here are some of the questions worth addressing:
- Are you writing?
- What have you written since the last meeting?
- Have your writing goals changed?
- Have you updated your vision statement?
- Has anything about your book's content, theme or approach changed?
- What challenges and/or distractions have you overcome?
- What's happening with your agent/publisher submission?

- What's new with your self-publishing venture?
- What other successes and achievements can you identify and celebrate, however seemingly minor?

Do your best to keep each contribution brief. This is not a time for mutual therapy, nor is it a time to make others feel guilty if they have done little since your last meeting. It's a time for accountability, kudos and support. You want to keep time available for either #2 or #3...or both.

2. WRITING/SHARING

Some groups like to use these get-togethers as an opportunity to write. If your group is one of those, set aside sufficient time for writing.

Pick or adapt an exercise from this book or from one of my other books for writers, create an exercise geared specifically to group members' needs or use a track from my *Voice of the Muse Companion* recording. Then set a timer for fifteen, twenty or thirty minutes and write.

Once everyone has finished, allow whoever wants to share what they have written that opportunity. Make sure everyone is familiar with the points in "Reaching Out for Feedback" in the next chapter.

In the beginning, as you are getting to know each other and each other's work, focus more on general support than on detailed feedback.

3. SHARING EXISTING WORK

Some groups prefer to use these get-togethers as an opportunity to share existing work, especially work created since their previous meeting. As with #2, above, have everyone first commit to the points in "Reaching Out for Feedback" and consider delaying detailed feedback until you have had a chance to get to know each other.

4. ROTATION

Take turns moderating the circle, hosting the circle and, where appropriate, choosing and leading the exercises.

5. FREQUENCY

Agree to meet regularly, at least monthly.

6. NUMBERS

Keep the size of your group small enough so that everyone who wants to has an opportunity to check in at every meeting and to share their work — if not at every meeting, then at every second or third meeting.

7. Atmosphere

For in-person get-togethers, create a space and ambience that is conducive to creativity and support, one that is quiet and where you and your fellow members won't be disturbed. Consider playing meditative music as people arrive to set the mood. People bond well over food, so many groups incorporate regular or occasional potlucks into their get-togethers.

If you are meeting via videoconference, urge all members to stay focused on your virtual circle by quitting all browsers, email programs and unnecessary applications and by muting all sounds unrelated to the group experience.

Under both scenarios, have all participants mute their cellphones, unplug their landlines and keep all other potentially distracting noise to a minimum.

If writing is part of your meeting, ensure that all laptop/tablet notifications and other sounds are switched off. Consider, too, using contemplative music during writing time, but poll your members first, as some people might prefer silence.

Remember, your Voice of the Muse Writers' Circle is designed to get you writing, keep you writing and support you in your book-birthing endeavors. Remember, too, that creativity at its best is a joyful experience. Write…and have fun.

Reaching Out for Feedback

You'll notice in the previous chapter that I avoided the popular term "critiquing group" in describing my writers' circles. Words like "criticism" and "critiquing" tend to start from the premise that something is wrong with the work being discussed. That's hardly an approach that fosters creativity.

I prefer to begin by assuming that more things are right than wrong with an author's work and to encourage comments that build writers up based on their successes rather than those that tear them down by focusing on their flaws. To me "feedback" carries with it the potential for that more supportive response. I especially like the *Roget's* synonym for feedback: "sympathetic vibration."

What follows are two sets of guidelines to assist you as you both reach out for feedback and respond to those who turn to you for your comments on their work.

The Seven Be's of Empowered Feedback

Others' views of your work can either be helpful or disruptive. How do you ensure the former? By following these seven "Be's" when sharing your manuscript with *anyone*.

1. Be Protective

Seek out only those people and situations that will support you in birthing your book. Never assume that those closest to you will be the most supportive. Often, without intending to hurt you, they are the most critical. When someone asks to read your book-in-progress, always use your discernment before responding and don't be shy about saying no.

2. Be Open

Don't let fear make you overprotective and prevent you from sharing your work and vision. Be open to outside perceptions, comments and responses, even as you exercise your discernment in determining which of them is relevant at any particular stage in your journey with your book.

3. Be Aware

To everything there is a season. At different stages in your book-birthing, you will be ready to hear different things from different people. Respect where you are and seek only the type and depth of feedback that you are prepared to receive and integrate. Recognize when you are at your most raw and respect that, too. As always, discernment is key.

4. Be Clear

Be clear within yourself about the type of feedback that you require and desire at this stage on your journey with your book. For example:
- Do you want to know what emotions your book evokes? Whether your reader found it funny? Touching? Convincing? Compelling? Original?
- Do you want to know whether the reader found your descriptions, imagery or settings vivid? Credible?
- If your book is a memoir, do you want friends or relatives to compare your version of events with theirs? Don't forget Be #1: Be Protective.
- Are you seeking line-by-line input? General comments only? Or maybe all you want is a pat on the back for having completed a first draft or a particularly challenging part of the book…or simply for having written.

It is up to you to determine what will support your book-birthing at this time and what might damage it, so…

5. Be Explicit

Once you have discerned the type and depth of feedback that is appropriate for you and your book, ask for it — clearly, directly and with neither apology nor equivocation. Don't be shy or embarrassed to make those needs known. Your reader cannot know how best to support you unless you do. If you are vague, hesitant or unclear, you open yourself to comments that you may not be ready to hear, comments that could feel hurtful or damaging, even if they are not intended to be so.

6. Be Strong

Know what you want and don't be afraid to speak up — lovingly, compassionately and, again, without apology — when you are not getting it, or when you are getting something you didn't ask for. This is your book and your creative journey. It's up to you to seek out what will help and support you as you birth your book and bring it to completion. In this, you are not only training yourself, you are training your friends, family and fellow writers to provide feedback in supportive ways and to seek it for themselves in empowered ways.

7. Be Discerning

Deep inside, you know your book's strengths and weaknesses. Tap into that inner knowingness and rely on it to discern which comments it is wisest to ignore and which support you and serve your book at this stage in its development and yours.

Remember that the words on your page are an expression of you but they are not you. Negative comments, whether intentionally cruel or not, have no power to harm or stifle you, unless you allow yourself to be hurt or blocked.

Explorations

Ask yourself these questions and don't think about the answers. Let them emerge freely and honestly…on the Muse Stream, where appropriate:

- How can I be clearer within myself about the feedback I need and with others about the feedback I am seeking?
- How can I be more discerning in who I turn to for feedback?
- Where have I been burnt in the past when seeking feedback? How can I avoid that in the future?
- How can I be more respectful of my book's needs and my own when seeking feedback?
- How can I be more discriminating in determining which feedback to take to heart and which to dismiss?

The Seven Be's of Compassionate Feedback

Before you pass any part of your book to friends, relatives or fellow writers for feedback, ask them to read and commit to these seven "Be's."

1. Be Open-Minded

You needn't agree with the author's views, beliefs or point of view in order to offer constructive feedback. Nor is it your place to comment on them, unless asked. Respect the author's approach and opinions. If you don't feel that you can, you are not the right person to be providing feedback.

2. Be Constructive

The only reason to offer feedback is to support the author and his or her book. This is not a test of your ability to pick out errors or flaws in the manuscript, nor is it an opportunity to criticize the author's choices. Don't be judgmental. Be openhearted. Don't be smart. Be gentle. Don't show off. Be fair.

3. Be Balanced

Always begin with the positive — with what you like about the book or excerpt, with its strengths, with what works for you, with what you admire or respect. With that foundation of support, offer your *constructive* comments, framing whatever you say with respect and compassion and honoring the parameters the author set out when asking you for feedback.

4. Be Specific

You are at your most helpful when you can offer examples from the text of what works and what doesn't. Be concrete. Be clear. Be fair.

5. Be Respectful

Give only the type and level of feedback the writer has sought. If there are other elements of the manuscript that you would like to comment on, ask permission. Respect the answer you get.

6. Be Nurturing

Sometimes all a writer needs is praise for having written. Avoid the kind of question Nora Barnacle is said to have asked husband and *Ulysses* author James Joyce: "Why don't you write books people can read?"

7. Be Compassionate

Honor the Golden Rule of Feedback: "Speak unto others in the manner you would have them speak unto you." Put yourself in the writer's shoes and offer feedback as you would *honestly* prefer to receive it.

Explorations

Ask yourself these questions and don't think about the answers. Let them emerge freely and honestly…on the Muse Stream, where appropriate:
- How can I listen more clearly to the nature of the feedback that has been requested of me?
- How can I be more explicit and specific in the feedback I offer?
- How can I be more respectful of the book and its author, offering feedback that doesn't show how smart I am but, instead, serves the needs and growth of the author and his or her book?

Rising Above Rejection

*I cannot read your M.S. three or four times. Not even one time.
Only one look, only one look is enough.
Hardly one copy would sell here.
Hardly one. Hardly one.*
PUBLISHER ARTHUR C. FIFIELD TO GERTRUDE STEIN, 1912

Few are the writers who never experience rejection (see the next chapter, "Rejected? You're Not the Only One!"). When an agent or publisher passes on your book, regardless of the reason, here are six ways to ease you through and past the pain.

1. REAL MEN CRY; REAL WOMEN CRY TOO

Don't bottle up your feelings. Feel what you feel. All of it. Cry. Curse. Yell. Scream. Throw things. Throw up. Then get past the rejection and move on.

2. WRITE YOUR FEELINGS

Powerful emotions birth powerful writing. If you're writing fiction, channel all your emotions into one of your characters — if not as part of this book, then as part of another. You're writing nonfiction? Release all your humiliation, anger, frustration, pain and despair onto the pages of your *Birthing Your Book* journal.

3. TAKE WRITER'S REVENGE

Write a scene where you subject whoever rejected you to something unspeakably hideous and horrific. It's the writer's equivalent of sticking pins into a voodoo doll. This scene will likely never make it into any of your books, but you will have more fun writing it than you ever ought to admit.

4. LOOK FOR THE SILVER LINING

It sounds clichéd but it remains true: Every experience, however emotionally debilitating, contains within it the seeds of something positive.

You may not be able to see the redemptive value of this rejection today, and that's fine. But once the pain has begun to subside, be open to a flash of insight that will reveal the silver lining around your storm cloud of rejection.

5. Look For The Spark Of Truth

It doesn't happen often, but your rejection letter could include reasons for the turndown, other than the standard "does not meet our needs at this time." If someone has taken the time to offer feedback, pay attention to it; use the discernment we talk about in "Reaching Out for Feedback" to determine whether it highlights real weaknesses that it would serve you to address in a new draft.

6. Keep Writing

Don't let one rejection — or one hundred or one hundred thousand — stop you. Keep writing and keep seeking out ways to become a better writer.

Explorations

Ask yourself these questions and don't think about the answers. Let them emerge freely and honestly…on the Muse Stream, where appropriate:
- How in the past have I handled rejection or negative feedback in unhealthy ways?
- How can I handle my next rejection in a more healthy, productive way than I did the last one?
- Can I refuse to let criticism or rejection stop me from moving forward with this book or with any other of my writing projects?
- If I am unable to get an agent or a publishing deal, can I trust that there may be other reasons why I was called to write this book? Can I be okay with that? (See "Your Book, Your Journey" in Section 11.)

Try This

Has discouragement or fear of failure slowed or halted your creative output? If you are reading these words today, it's because writing and creative expression are important to you. Sure, you want to be published. Who doesn't? But what's more important: a lucrative publishing contract or the opportunity to release onto the page the stirrings of your soul? Yes, both would be nice. Yet the former cannot happen unless you are writing. So write!

Rejected? You're Not the Only One!

Author Madeleine L'Engle received two years' worth of rejections from twenty-six publishers for her novel *A Wrinkle in Time*, which, once it was finally published in 1962, went on to win major awards and be translated into more than a dozen languages. It's still in print and still popular.

Toward the end of that demoralizing two-year period, L'Engle covered up her typewriter and decided to give up, on *A Wrinkle in Time* and on writing. Moments later L'Engle had an idea for a new novel — about failure. In a flash, she was back at her typewriter.

"That night," as she explained thirty years later in a PBS documentary, "I wrote in my journal, 'I'm a writer. That's who I am. That's what I am. That's what I have to do — even if I'm never, ever published again.' And I had to take seriously the fact that I might never, ever be published again. … It's easy to say I'm a writer now, but I said it when it was hard to say. And I meant it."

The book world is littered with similar rejections…

- J.K. Rowling was declined by a dozen publishers before Bloomsbury embraced the first Harry Potter novel. Rowling and her books have gone on to make literary and film history.
- Surgeon H. Richard Hornberger struck out twenty-one times with his first novel, written under the name Richard Hooker, before William Morrow picked it up. Today *M*A*S*H* is a film and TV legend.
- Theodore Geisel's first book as Dr. Seuss was turned down twenty-seven times before landing a publishing contract. Geisel ultimately won a pair of Oscars and Emmys, as well as a Pulitzer and a Peabody Award.
- Stephen King, discouraged after *Carrie*'s thirtieth rejection, tossed the manuscript into the trash. Fortunately, his wife retrieved it: *Carrie* sold more than one million copies in its first year and King is now ranked as one of the top-selling authors of all time.
- Jack Canfield and Mark Victor Hansen had Rowling, Hornberger, King and Geisel beat: The original *Chicken Soup for the Soul* book was rejected by more than one hundred publishers ("nobody wants to read a book of short little stories") before it launched a multimillion-dollar franchise, selling more than 80 million copies in 37 countries.

There's more…

- Publishing giant Alfred A. Knopf rejected Jack Kerouac's *On the Road*, dismissing it as a huge, sprawling and inconclusive novel that would attract small sales and garner indignant reviews. Knopf also rejected George Orwell's *Animal Farm* ("it is impossible to sell animal stories in the U.S.A."), as well as Sylvia Plath ("there certainly isn't enough genuine talent for us to take notice"), Anne Frank, Isaac Bashevis Singer ("it's Poland and the rich Jews again") and Vladimir Nabokov.
- Kurt Vonnegut, William Faulkner, Judy Blume, Jorge Luis Borges ("utterly untranslatable"), Norman Mailer ("this will set publishing back twenty-five years"), James Joyce and D.H. Lawrence also received multiple rejections before finally getting a yes.
- Other classic rebuffs? Richard Bach's *Jonathan Livingston Seagull*, William Golding's *Lord of the Flies*, John le Carré's *The Spy Who Came in from the Cold* ("you're welcome to le Carré — he hasn't got any future"), Joseph Heller's *Catch-22*, Neale Donald Walsch's *Conversations with God*, Kenneth Grahame's *The Wind in the Willows* ("an irresponsible holiday story"), the original "Tarzan of the Apes" story by Edgar Rice Burroughs and F. Scott Fitzgerald's *The Great Gatsby* ("you'd have a decent book if you'd get rid of that Gatsby character").

10. Living Your Book

*Miracles are not contrary to nature,
but only contrary to what we know about nature.*
St. Augustine

To ask an author who hopes to be a serious writer if his work is autobiographical is like asking a spider where he buys his thread.
Robertson Davies, novelist

The Story Knows Best

In June 1997, three months after the end of the Georgian Bay retreat I describe in Book-Birthing Rule #7, I embarked on an odyssey whose consequences I could never have predicted...or imagined. I had been back living in Toronto for only a short while when a voice in my heart urged me to pack all I owned (not a lot) into the back of my Dodge Caravan and head west.

At earlier times in my life, I would have doubted the message, questioned my sanity. On that sunny morning, I knew my only choice was to trust and follow my heart.

For three months I journeyed. I traveled north and west from Toronto along the rugged, forested shores of Lake Huron and Lake Superior, then south and west, crossing Minnesota, North Dakota, South Dakota, Wyoming, Montana, Idaho and Oregon. From the Oregon coast, I slipped south into California, then shot back east, across Nevada and Utah, before dropping into northern Arizona.

As I traveled, I never planned my next stop. When I tried, my plans were nearly always thwarted by some seemingly outside force. Mostly, I let my heart control the steering wheel and I followed wherever it took me.

It was a magically transformative experience, though not without stress, for it was difficult at times to surrender fully. Part of me longed to plot an itinerary, to know where I would drive the next week, to know where I would end up. The greater, more courageous part of me trusted in the infinite wisdom of the journey.

Through all the unexpected stops, unanticipated detours and unpredicted forays into uncharted territory, all I could do was trust in each moment and believe that the story I was living would reveal itself — through the living of it.

It did. Magnificently.

On the morning of the full moon in September, after ninety days of journeying, I drove into Sedona, Arizona. I expected this to be another whistle stop on the road to wherever. Instead, one week grew to two, one month to seven. Before I knew it, I had a new country and a new wife, and a new baby was on the way.

Had I given my brain-mind the control it sought, I might never have left Toronto, might never have launched a journey that gifted me with so much richness.

Part of what prepared me for this odyssey was *The MoonQuest*, the novel whose early drafts I had already written much as I lived that journey: moment by moment and word by word, ignorant of the outcome but trusting that one would emerge.

When we surrender to our heart-mind, trusting that the outcome will be more wondrous than anything we could consciously imagine, it always is.

As you move forward with your book, let your pen carry you as my Dodge Caravan did me — in trust and surrender. Let it carry you into and through the story you didn't know you knew as, breath by breath, you move toward an outcome that has yet to reveal itself.

As I write in *The Voice of the Muse: Answering the Call to Write*, "All I can do — all we can ever do, in writing as in life — is trust in the story. It has never let me down before. Truly, the story knows best."

Try This

In today's writing, notice all the times your mind contradicts your intuition, when what you think your book should be tries to edge (or leap) ahead of the word you are writing. Be aware as that controlling part of yourself reaches forward to find out what's coming next, to figure out where you're headed, to predict how it will end.

Notice when this happens, but don't judge or punish yourself. Simply return your focus to the word of the moment. Return to it gently, lovingly, reassuringly. And continue to let your book unfold, in the moment, keystroke by keystroke and word by word.

Explorations

Writing a book is an act of pilgrimage. We set out on a journey, often intent on a particular direction and destination. Yet if we are true to our art and to our heart, we free the book to carry us where it will. The resulting journey is one that reveals to us not only the story we are writing but the story we are living.

When we listen for the stories that move through us, we also discover the story that is us.

- How has this book you are writing been a pilgrimage?
- What has it taught you — about yourself, about your work, about the world?

Write about that without thinking too deeply about it. Instead, let the Muse Stream reveal to you what you didn't know you knew.

Mark David's Rules for Living a Creative Life

A few years after creating my original "rules" for writing, I revised and updated them — not to alter their essence but to align them with an analogous set of rules that I had crafted for living. I have blended them here into a single set because the rules are so similar. Why is that? Because the same precepts you apply to your creativity work the same way in the rest of your life. Because in writing your book, you are also living your book.

RULE #1: THERE ARE NO RULES

How can there be rules when creativity and life are about blazing your own trail, breaking new ground, breaking old rules? Living a creative life means there can never be a single right way that works for everyone all the time. There is no universal wrong way either, only the way that works for you today, so…

RULE #2: BE IN THE MOMENT

What works for you today may not work tomorrow or ever again, so you might as well live in the present moment. Focus on *now* — on the breath you are breathing and the word you are writing. The next will always come if you don't worry about it…if you let it.

RULE #3: LISTEN TO YOUR HEART

Your heart speaks with the voice of God and the voice of your Muse (or whatever you call that divine/creative/infinite intelligence we all carry within us). Listen and trust that intuitive voice without judgment, censorship or second-guessing. It's wiser than you are and knows, better than you ever will, both the story you are living and the story you are writing.

RULE #4: LOVE YOURSELF AND YOUR WORDS

Treat every aspect of yourself and every draft of your writing as you would treat your child or best friend: with love, compassion and respect. Don't beat yourself up, and don't diminish or denigrate yourself or your work, for any reason.

Rule #5: Be Vulnerable

Share your pain and your passion — as you live and in your writing. That's what makes you human. That's what connects you with others, in both your life and your art. Or, as I put it elsewhere in this book: "Walk the earth naked, clothed only in your truth."

Rule #6: Strip Off Your Straitjackets

Don't live or write according to others' expectations…or according to your own preconceptions. Free yourself to follow the path that is uniquely yours. Free your words to take on the form that is uniquely theirs. Surrender to the resulting gifts and let yourself be amazed by them.

Rule #7: Abandon Ruts and Rote

Kick free of your ruts. Ditch your routines. If you're feeling stuck, shake things up by making different choices. If you're paralyzed by the fear that you will make a "wrong" choice, stop worrying and make any choice. In your writing, write something, *anything*, to get started or to keep going. Find ways to keep moving with the current of life and to keep flowing in the stream of creation.

Rule #8: Surrender

You're not in charge, so abandon control, get out of the way and let your story have its way with you — the story you are living as much as the story you are writing.

Rule #9: Commit to Your Passion

Find your passion and embrace it. Passionately. Then commit to that passion, unconditionally.

Rule #10: Embrace Imperfection

Perfection is no more possible in your writing than it is in the rest of your life, so embrace the perfect imperfection of both your creativity and your humanity. Strive for excellence, not perfection.

Rule #11: Lighten Up

Don't take your life or art too seriously. Just as you don't censor your pain (see Rule #5), don't censor your joy. Giggle, laugh, guffaw, play. Have fun as you create and as you live.

Rule #12: Empower Yourself For Success

This is your life and your creative journey. Don't let anyone else take charge of them. Don't let anyone else tell you how to live and express them (or how not to live and express them). Empower yourself by defining success on your terms, not on anyone else's. Then set easy goals and meet them. In doing so, you will set yourself up for success not for failure — in both your life and your art.

Rule #13: There Are No Rules

There are no rules. None. Never.

Explorations

Ask yourself these questions and don't think about the answers. Let them emerge freely and honestly…on the Muse Stream, where appropriate:

- How many of these "rules" now govern my writing and my life, at least to some degree? (Be honest.)
- Which rules am I resisting in my writing? In my life?
- How have my life issues affected my creativity? How have my writing issues affected my life?
- Where can I lighten up and loosen up to live more creatively? To write more freely?

Try This

Write about the connections you are aware of between your life and your creativity. Use the above rules if that's helpful. Then, on the Muse Stream, explore those connections that lie beneath your conscious awareness and see what you discover. And see what, through your discoveries, you can begin to transform — in your writing and in your life.

Trust. Let Go. Leap.

Legendary science fiction author Ray Bradbury once said that, for him, writing was about leaping off cliffs and trusting that he would sprout wings on the way down. In many ways, what Bradbury describes is the way of The Fool in the Tarot: that surrendered leap of faith into the void that alchemically transforms into art something that, in the moment, appears to make no sense.

It can be a terrifying way to write. It can also be a terrifying way to live. Ultimately, though, it is always satisfying. It certainly has been for me — both terrifying and satisfying!

And even though it has meant living and writing without a net, those wings Bradbury talks about have never failed to appear for me. They first showed themselves two decades ago in the wake of a nightmare. In it, I was clinging to the roof ledge of a fifties-style office tower while an inner voice kept urging me to jump. I didn't dare. I couldn't.

Later, as I had done with other dreams, I took this disturbing image into meditation and in each of three sessions unsuccessfully tried to let go of that old structure. By my fourth attempt, the gripping sensation felt so painful that I just did it: I unhooked my fingers from the stonework in my mind, fully expecting to plummet to the pavement in a messy splat.

Instead, I found myself floating down, feather-like, until I landed safely in what I could then only describe as the arms of God.

Before he died, Apple's Steve Jobs said, "You have to trust in something — your gut, destiny, life, karma, whatever. This approach has never let me down, and it has made all the difference in my life."

Jobs was right. That "something," however you choose to name it, has never let me down either. Over the years, in both my writing and my life, I have taken many Fool-like leaps that defy both logic and convention. And although I have experienced fear along the way, the rewards have always surpassed the discomfort.

I would not be living in the United States right now, for example, had I resisted the call I describe earlier in this section, in "The Story Knows Best," to hit the road with with everything I owned in the back of my car.

A similar if tenfold-longer journey in the decade that followed brought me to New Mexico and allowed me to gift myself and the world with, now, eleven published books.

Over the years I have discovered that once I commit to the highest possible path and purpose, a trinity of principles is always at play:

>TRUST
>
>LET GO
>
>LEAP

First, I *trust* the voice of my deepest heart and my Muse — Steve Job's "something" and the voice of what I sometimes call "infinite mind." Next, I *let go* all resistance (which doesn't mean that I'm not afraid, nor does it mean that I have to know how whatever I'm being called to do is possible). Finally, I *leap* into the void — just like that Fool in the Tarot — only to discover the ever-present miracle of Ray Bradbury's wings.

Miracles are at-hand in every moment of our lives. It's our limited vision that prevents us from seeing them. It's our limited sense of what is possible that prevents us from believing in them. It's our fear that prevents us from embracing them.

Those miracles are available to us as magnificently in our writing as they are in the rest of our lives. What else would you call the logic-defying cohesion of *The Q'ntana Trilogy*, each of its stories written with little or no conscious notion of plot or sequel, except as its words moved through me onto the page?

Trust.

Let Go.

Leap.

In writing as in my life, it always works.

11. Parting Words

If man is created in God's image,
it can only mean that he is created creative.
FREDERICK FRANCK, ARTIST

Stories never really end,
even if the books like to pretend they do.
Stories always go on.
CORNELIA FUNKE, NOVELIST

It's Time to Live the Dream

What's your dream for your book? Know that whatever it is, however improbable it may seem in this moment, it's not impossible.

Nearly every success story begins with an "impossible" dream. Nearly every "overnight success" was years in the making.

What about your dream for your book? Have you abandoned it? Stuffed it in the back of a drawer because it seems so unreachable?

Open that drawer. Reach your hand in. Gently. Touch it. Reconnect with it. Reconnect with yourself.

Have you started the book you have always seen yourself writing? The book that brought you to this book?

No?

Then now is the time to begin to put your dream into action. It doesn't matter whether you can give it five minutes a day or five hours. It doesn't even matter whether you know in this moment what your book is about or where it will take you.

Every journey begins with a single step. Every book begins with a single word. One word. Any word.

Write that word. Now.

Open your heart again. Open your heart to the vision. Open your heart to the passion. Open your heart to yourself. Say yes to you!

Try This

Writing on the Muse Stream, explore your dreams for your book. Deepen your awareness of the dreams you know about and discover the dreams that still lie hidden in your heart and unconscious mind. If you need help getting started, use this key phrase: "My dreams for my book are…"

Try This Too

Write on the Muse Stream from these opening sentences: "I am ready to live my dream. I am ready to write my book." Let this be a statement of commitment and part of your first step toward realizing the dream that is your book…a dream that is as realizable as you allow it to be.

You Are a Writer: A Guided Meditation

I include this meditation in all my books for writers because it's too easy, as creative artists working largely in isolation, to diminish both ourselves and our output and to forget that we are powerful and empowered creators. Read or listen to this meditation when you feel doubt...when you feel less-than...when you don't believe that you will ever be able to complete your book...when you question whether you are even a writer. In those moments, let the words and spirit of what follows remind you that you *are* a writer of power, passion, strength and courage. For committing to the act of writing a book takes courage...immeasurable courage. And you are doing it!

ALLOW 5 MINUTES FOR THIS MEDITATIVE EXPERIENCE.

Close your eyes and take a few deep breaths as you relax and listen...

You are a writer. You are a writer of power, passion, strength and, yes, courage. For writing is an act of courage. Acknowledge that courage, the courage that got you to this point...having written. Having written today, if you have. Having written just now, if you have.

You are a writer. Breathe into that. Breathe into the release you felt as the pen flowed across the page, as letters formed into words, words stretched into sentences and sentences began to fill your pages.

Breathe into the freedom, the vibrancy, the love. Breathe into the knowledge and knowingness that you can do it again. And again. And again. And again.

You are a writer. What you write is powerful. What you write is vibrant. What you write, whatever you believe in this moment, is luminous.

Trust that to the best of your ability, in this moment. Acknowledge the writer you are, in this moment. Breathe into that.

Breathe out judgment. Breathe out fear. Breathe out not-good-enoughs. Breathe out comparisons. What others have written does not matter. What you have written is all that matters now, in this moment. It is perfect...in this moment. Know that. Trust that. Breathe into that.

If you don't feel ready to read what you have written from that place of trust, discernment and compassion, set it aside. Set it aside for a time — until you arrive at a place of more clarity, more objectivity, more self-love.

Don't avoid reading it, but nor do you need to rush into it. Either way, for now know that you are a writer. A writer writes. That's what you have done. You have written.

>You are a *writer.*
>
>You *are* a writer.
>
>*You* are a writer.

You've heard the words. Now speak them with me…

>I am a *writer.*
>
>I *am* a writer.
>
>*I* am a writer.

Speak them again and again and again, knowing them to be true.
Speak them again, feeling the truth in them.
Speak them again, for they are true.

- *My recording of this meditation is included — along with ten other, equally inspiring tracks — on "The Voice of the Muse Companion: Guided Meditations for Writers." Look for it on Amazon, iTunes and Google Play and from other online music sellers.*

Your Book, Your Journey

Unlike in my twenties when, as a freelance journalist my writing was skilled and craftsmanlike and written from the surface, my current creations rise up from profound, gut-wrenching inner places that challenge me as little else in my life ever has. In metaphysical terms, they are "energy activations" that force me to face my deepest fears and impel me to trust more fully and surrender more completely than I sometimes believe possible.

All my books come from that place. Even *Birthing Your Book*, which I expected to be among the easiest of my books to write, has found ways to test me.

To be clear, the writing itself is not difficult, thanks to the Muse Stream. No, what challenges me are the tectonic shifts of inner revolution — outer, too, sometimes — that are inevitable byproducts of this kind of writing journey.

Even on those days when I grumble and grouse and raise my voice to the heavens with a *God, I wish I was finished with this book!*, I must acknowledge that the real reason I write is to experience those tectonic shifts, to uncover the hidden depths I write about in "Write What You Know?" (Section 5), to discover what it is I believe, to remember all that I have forgotten.

I could insist that I write to engage, impassion, motivate, touch and inspire *you*…and that would be true. I do want my books to accomplish all those things. But the only way I can I do that for you is if I first do it for myself. How? By surrendering to the leaps of faith that this journey of writing from the heart demands — in other words, by following my Rule #2 for both birthing your book and living a creative life: Be in the moment.

When writing a book, we like to think that we are writing toward an outcome — toward a completed book, a publishing contract, great reviews, a global readership. But in writing as in life, our destination is nothing but another new beginning, the start of another journey. And the journey is life itself.

If we turn our backs on that journey to focus on outcomes and destinations, we turn our backs on life and on all the gifts that each moment — and each word — has to offer us. Some of those gifts may cause us discomfort, may cause us to question long-held attitudes, beliefs and ways of being. That's a good thing.

I noted early on in *Birthing Your Book* that writing is an act of transformation. You cannot expect to be the same person at the end of this book you are birthing as you were at the beginning. If you were, what would have been the point of writing it?

Acknowledge that you are the first and most important audience for your book. Surrender to its wizardry and to the alchemical changes it will wring out of you. Revel in those tectonic shifts. Celebrate the journey. Let your life and your book be one. Become the book you are writing. Write the book you are becoming.

Explorations

Ask yourself these questions and don't think about the answers. Let them emerge freely and honestly…on the Muse Stream, where appropriate:
- What is my relationship with my book today? Has it altered over time? If so, how?
- What alchemical changes or tectonic shifts have I experienced through my journey with this book? What changes or shifts am I continuing to experience?
- Do I know why I am writing this book? Are my reasons different today than they were when I started out? If so, in what ways?

Endings and Beginnings

Do you remember the questions I asked when you first opened *Birthing Your Book*? I invited you to note where you were with your writing and with your book as you prepared to join me on this journey. Then I encouraged you to seal those thoughts in an envelope and forget about them.

It is now time to open the envelope and read what you wrote, reacquainting yourself with where you believed yourself to be last week, last month or last year…whenever you started this book.

Do you recognize the writer you were?

Are you surprised now by what you wrote then?

Has anything changed?

Has everything changed?

Turn over your card/paper or get a fresh one, close your eyes, take a few deep breaths and whisk yourself back in time…back to the day you first opened this book…back to the day you wrote those words.

As you continue to focus on your breath, allow yourself to journey forward from that day to this one. Re-experience all you experienced through that time, recalling both fears and flowerings, terrors and triumphs, as you let those feeling-memories swirl through you.

Then, taking a few more deep breaths, allow a word or phrase to float up into your awareness, one that describes who and where you are at this moment of endings and new beginnings. Don't judge it. Surrender to it, whatever it is, then write it under today's date next to the question, "Where am I now?"

Next, write a few lines on the Muse Stream describing where you are today with your writing and your book, using these questions as prompts:

- What did I accomplish and achieve over the course of my time with *Birthing Your Book*?
- Who/where am I at the end of this book that I wasn't at the beginning?
- What has changed for me and for my book since I wrote those first words all those pages ago?
- Where do I choose to go from here?

Wherever that is, take your first step toward that goal.

Do it.

Now.

More from Mark David Gerson

The MoonQuest: The Q'ntana Trilogy, Book I

Prologue

Na'an came to me in a dream this night. It was early. I had not been in bed long and the night was newly dark.

"It is time," she said, "time to fix The MoonQuest on parchment."

I was gladdened to see her after so many seasons, but I was not cheered by the message she bore. I tried to engage her in other discourse, but she was single-minded as only a Tikkan dreamwalker can be.

"It is not for me to boast of my exploits," I argued. "Others have sung them. Let them continue."

"No," she said, and her silver tresses shimmered as she shook her head. "It is your story to tell. It is for you to fix it in ink, to set the truth down for all to read."

I tried to resist, to shut Na'an's words from my heart, to return to the dreamless sleep that preceded her appearance. But Tikkan speak only what we know in our hearts to be true, and my heart would not close to her even as my mind longed to. Only by forcing my eyes open and my body to this table was I able to banish her milk-white face from my mind's eye. Only by letting my quill rasp across the blank parchment have I stilled her voice.

But my quill hovers over oceans of emptiness. I don't know what to write, where to begin. The story has so many beginnings and no clear ending. As a bard, as Elderbard, I am trained to know how to weave disparate elements into a tapestry of word and song that brings light and meaning to life. When recounting others' stories, I have no difficulty. The tales unfurl from my tongue as if by magic, as if M'nor herself were singing through me.

Na'an says it is my story. Perhaps she is right. Is that why the words come so reluctantly? So many seasons of storytelling and still I hesitate. Of all the stories to stick in my throat, how ironic that it should be The MoonQuest, a tale of the freeing of story itself.

You see how confused I am? I have not even introduced myself. My truth name is Toshar and I am old, so old that most who knew me by that name have passed on to other worlds.

Toshar… Even I have forgotten the boy who was Toshar, the youth who embarked on The MoonQuest all those seasons ago.

They call me Ko'lar now, the ancient word for Elderbard. It is a sign of honor and respect, but it separates me from the youth I was.

Perhaps Na'an is right. Perhaps it is time to bring back Toshar, to allow the boy I was to touch the man I have become, the man I will soon cease to be. Soon it will be time to release the ageless spirit from this aged body and move on to other realms, set off on other journeys. I have seen it and I welcome it. But it cannot be mine until I have told this story. Na'an insists.

She speaks, even as I sit here in full wakefulness, staring at the shadows cast by my flickering taper. Now, they loom, large and menacing. Now, they flit and flutter in delicate dance. I see it all now, in the leap of light against dark. The shadows will tell me the story and I will write what I see. I will write until my fingers and beard are black with ink. I will write until the story is told.

Only then will I be free to continue my journey. Only then will my daughter, Q'nta, be free to continue hers. She is nearly ready. Ryolan Ò Garan taught her well, taught her the lessons of The MoonQuest. Soon she will live them through my words and will be free to assume the mantle of her birthright, according to the ancient orders of succession:

> *From father to daughter, mother to son*
> *The mantle passes, the Balance is done*

I was an exception to the Law of Balance, a law as old as the land itself. But those were exceptional times, the darkest of ages, in a land where "once upon a time" was a forbidden phrase and fact the only legal tender.

That was the land I was born into, a land of slaughtered bards, a land dulled and divided by fear. That was Q'ntana, and this is its story, and mine…a story that begins once upon a time.

Acts of Surrender: A Writer's Memoir

Genesis

I began this book in mid-2009, shortly after having finished a first draft of *The StarQuest*, the second novel in my *Q'ntana Trilogy*. I did not want to write a memoir and, as Toshar did with Na'an in *The MoonQuest*, I kept arguing about it with my ever-insistent Muse. Who, I asked repeatedly, would care about my personal stories? Perhaps, had I known back then that the title would be *Acts of Surrender*, I might have seen the cosmic joke and given in more gracefully. Perhaps, had I seen the parallel with *The MoonQuest* sooner, I might have been more pliant. Muses, though, are nothing if not persistent and, in the end my resistance proved futile... as it always does.

Ironically, the challenge I faced when beginning *Acts of Surrender* was similar to the one I had encountered with *The MoonQuest*: I did not know the story. Oh, I knew my story or, at least, my version of it. What I didn't know was the book's shape or its theme. How could I begin to write without knowing these things? Without knowing these things, how would I be able to condense more than a half century's living into a compelling, manageably sized narrative?

An outline was out of the question. As I often confess in my talks and workshops, I have never managed the art of the outline. Even in high school, when I was required to submit one with an essay, I wrote the essay first and crafted the outline afterward. Without knowing it, I had already adopted a writing philosophy I would not consciously connect with for nearly two decades: Just start and let the story reveal itself to you in the writing.

Could I do that in a nonfiction memoir with the same success I had achieved in novel and screenplay? Could I trust that my memoir was its own entity separate from the story I had lived and that it knew more about itself than I did? Could I surrender to that superior wisdom? Perhaps the more appropriate question was, How could I not?

As you will read in these pages, much of my life has been about growing into a place of surrender. To be clear, I don't use the word "surrender" to describe a demeaning or submissive stance. Rather, I acknowledge the existence of an infinite mind whose wisdom transcends my conscious thoughts, and I do my best to defer to it. This is not an energy that exists separate from me. It is not a white-bearded, white-robed gentleman peering down from on high. Whatever it is — and I don't pretend to have solved the theological/scientific question of the ages — it is something that is both within me and of which I am part. Whatever it is, it is definitely smarter than I am, and *that* is where my surrender is directed.

Of course, I would have to write a book of my stories in the same way I had lived them: from a place of surrender, trusting that the story of my memoir would reveal itself to me in the writing of it, just as the story of my life has revealed itself to me in the living of it. In other words, how could *Acts of Surrender* be anything but another act of surrender?

CPSIA information can be obtained
at www.ICGtesting.com
Printed in the USA
LVHW081315040521
686456LV00011B/250